By |
and The

POLITICAL PHILOSOPHY

Summarized

Key Thinkers, Theories, and Debates on Power, Justice, and Freedom—From Plato to Postmodernism

West Agora Int

Timisoara 2025

WEST AGORA INT S.R.L.

All Rights Reserved

Copyright © WEST AGORA INT 2025

West Agora Int

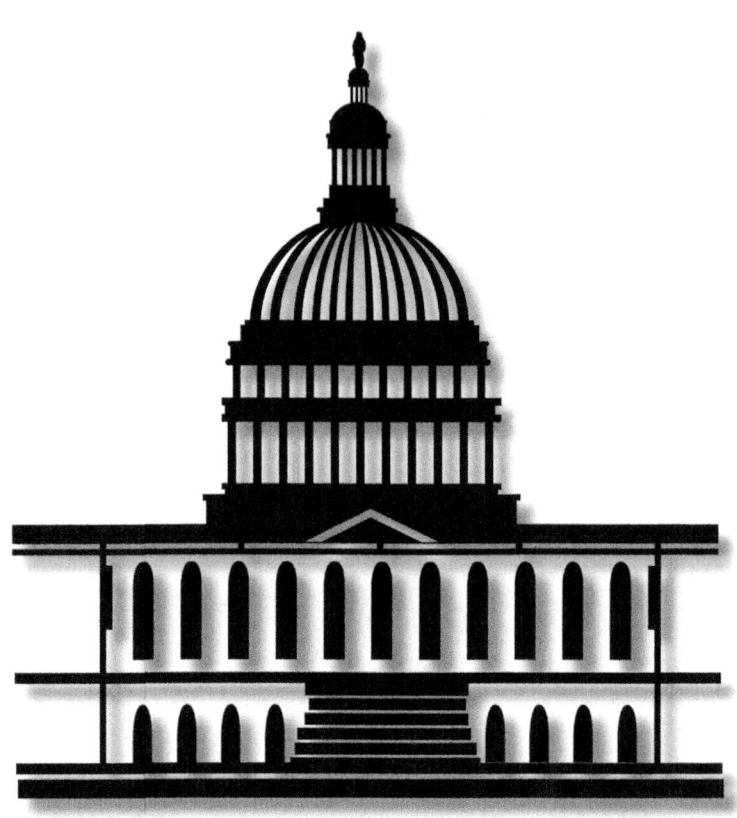

POLITICAL PHILOSOPHY Summarized
Copyright © 2025
West Agora Int

All rights reserved. No part of this book may be copied, reproduced, distributed, or transmitted in any form or by any means, including photocopying, recording, or other electronic or mechanical methods, without prior written permission from the publisher, except in the case of brief quotations used in a review, article, or scholarly critique.

This book is intended as a general resource and does not constitute professional advice. While every effort has been made to ensure the accuracy and completeness of the information contained herein, the author and publisher disclaim any liability or responsibility for errors, omissions, or outcomes arising from the use of this material.

Requests for permission or inquiries regarding this work may be directed to the publisher:

West Agora Int

All trademarks and registered trademarks appearing in this book are the property of their respective owners. Their inclusion does not imply any affiliation or endorsement by them.

Unauthorized reproduction or distribution of this book is strictly prohibited and may result in civil and criminal penalties under applicable copyright laws.

Published by West Agora Int
Edited by West Agora Int
Cover Art by West Agora Int

What is justice? Who should rule? Can power ever be legitimate?

For centuries, the greatest minds have wrestled with these questions—shaping nations, igniting revolutions, and defining the very fabric of society. From the ideal republic of Plato to the fiery critiques of Marx, from the ruthless realism of Machiavelli to the modern anxieties of surveillance and AI governance, Political Philosophy Summarized takes you on a gripping journey through the most powerful ideas that have shaped human civilization.

This is no dry academic textbook. It's a bold, accessible, and razor-sharp guide that distills the wisdom of history's greatest political thinkers into clear, compelling insights. Whether you're a student, a thinker, or simply someone who wants to understand the forces driving today's world, this book delivers everything you need to master political philosophy—without the fluff, jargon, or confusion.

Inside, you'll discover:
The battles of ideas that forged democracy, authoritarianism, and everything in between
The social contract theories that built the modern state—and the radical thinkers who rejected them
The philosophies of freedom and oppression, from John Stuart Mill to totalitarian regimes
The future of politics—technology, AI, climate change, and the next great ideological wars
If you want to think smarter about power, government, and the future of society, this is your essential guide.

Understand the past. Decipher the present. Shape the future.

TABLE OF CONTENTS

Political Philosophy Jargon..6
What is Political Philosophy?.. 15
The State and Its Justification... 20
Power, Authority, and Legitimacy... 25
Justice: The Core of Political Philosophy... 30
Liberty and Freedom.. 35
Equality and Rights..40
Ancient Greek Political Philosophy... 45
Roman and Medieval Political Thought..50
Machiavelli and Realpolitik... 55
Hobbes, Locke, and the Social Contract..59
Rousseau and the General Will.. 64
Liberalism: Classical vs. Modern.. 69
Marxism and Critiques of Capitalism... 74
Utilitarianism and Political Decision-Making....................................79
Libertarianism and Minimal Government.. 84
Conservatism and Tradition... 89
Theories of Democracy..94
Critiques of Democracy... 99
Totalitarianism and Authoritarianism... 105
Populism and the Crisis of Democracy... 110
The Role of Law in Politics..115
Political Economy and the State...120
Nationalism and Identity Politics.. 125
Imperialism and Colonialism.. 130
War, Peace, and International Relations...135
Feminist Political Thought..140
Multiculturalism and Political Pluralism... 145
Environmental Political Philosophy.. 150
Technology and Political Power... 155
Future of Political Philosophy.. 160
Conclusion: Why Political Philosophy Matters................................ 165
Further Reading...170

 Political Philosophy Jargon

Political philosophy, like any intellectual discipline, has developed a specialized vocabulary to articulate its key concepts, debates, and traditions. This glossary provides an essential reference for readers seeking to familiarize themselves with the fundamental terminology of political philosophy. Understanding these terms is crucial for grasping the nuances of political theory, analyzing historical texts, and engaging with contemporary debates.

A

Absolutism – A political system in which a single ruler or governing body holds unlimited and unquestionable power, often justified by divine right or necessity.

Anarchism – A political philosophy that rejects the necessity of the state, advocating for a stateless society based on voluntary cooperation and self-governance. Key thinkers include Mikhail Bakunin, Peter Kropotkin, and Emma Goldman.

Aristocracy – A form of government in which power is held by a privileged class or ruling elite, often justified by claims of noble birth, wisdom, or virtue.

Authority – The legitimate right to exercise power, often distinguished from mere coercion. Max Weber identified three types of authority: traditional, charismatic, and legal-rational.

B

Balance of Power – A principle in international relations theory that suggests stability is achieved when power is distributed among multiple states so that no single state dominates.

Bourgeoisie – A term from Marxist theory, referring to the capitalist class that owns the means of production and exploits the working class (proletariat).

Bureaucracy – A system of government or administration characterized by hierarchical organization, fixed rules, and impersonal decision-making. Max Weber analyzed bureaucracy as the defining feature of modern governance.

C

Capitalism – An economic and political system based on private ownership of the means of production and market-driven economies, often associated with liberalism and thinkers like Adam Smith and Friedrich Hayek.

Citizenship – The legal and political status of being a member of a state, with associated rights and responsibilities. Different models include liberal citizenship, republican citizenship, and cosmopolitan citizenship.

Civil Disobedience – The act of deliberate, nonviolent resistance to unjust laws, often associated with Henry David Thoreau, Mahatma Gandhi, and Martin Luther King Jr.

Civil Rights – The legal protections and freedoms that safeguard individuals from discrimination and government overreach, often associated with democratic governance.

Common Good – The idea that political arrangements should prioritize the well-being of the entire community, rather than serving narrow individual or class interests. This is central to Aristotle, Rousseau, and communitarian theorists.

Communism – A political and economic theory advocating for the abolition of private property and the establishment of a classless, stateless society. Karl Marx and Friedrich Engels laid its intellectual foundation in The Communist Manifesto.

Conservatism – A political philosophy emphasizing tradition, gradual change, and social stability. Key thinkers include Edmund

Burke, Michael Oakeshott, and Roger Scruton.

Contractarianism – The idea that society and political authority originate from a social contract. Hobbes, Locke, and Rousseau provided influential theories of contractarianism.

Cosmopolitanism – A political philosophy advocating for global citizenship and the moral duty to all human beings, regardless of national or cultural affiliation.

Coercion – The use of force or intimidation to compel obedience, often contrasted with legitimate authority.

D

Democracy – A system of government in which political power is vested in the people, either directly or through elected representatives. Major forms include direct democracy, representative democracy, and deliberative democracy.

Demagogue – A political leader who gains power by exploiting popular emotions, prejudices, and fears, often undermining democratic institutions.

Dialectical Materialism – A Marxist theory explaining historical development through class struggle and economic contradictions.

Distributive Justice – A concept in political philosophy concerned with how wealth, resources, and power should be allocated in a society. Major theorists include John Rawls and Robert Nozick.

Divine Right of Kings – A pre-modern theory that monarchs derive their authority directly from God, making their rule unquestionable.

E

Egalitarianism – The belief in equal rights and opportunities for all individuals, often in conflict with hierarchical or meritocratic systems.

Elitism – The idea that political power should be concentrated in the hands of a small, capable, or knowledgeable elite. Plato's philosopher-king and Schumpeter's elite theory of democracy reflect this perspective.

Empiricism – A philosophical method emphasizing experience and observation as the basis for knowledge, influencing political philosophy through figures like John Locke and David Hume.

Enlightenment – An intellectual movement emphasizing reason, individual rights, and scientific inquiry, laying the foundation for liberalism and modern democracy. Thinkers include Kant, Rousseau, and Voltaire.

F

Fascism – A far-right, authoritarian ideology that rejects democracy, promotes nationalism, and prioritizes state power and militarism. Associated with Mussolini and Hitler.

Federalism – A political system where power is divided between central and regional governments, seen in the United States and European Union.

Freedom of Speech – A core liberal principle protecting individuals' right to express opinions without government censorship, though debated in cases of hate speech and misinformation.

G

General Will – A concept from Jean-Jacques Rousseau, referring to the collective interests of a society that should guide governance, distinct from individual self-interest.

Globalization – The increasing interconnection of economies, cultures, and political systems, raising debates about sovereignty and economic inequality.

Government Legitimacy – The justification of political authority, often debated in terms of consent, effectiveness, and moral justification.

H

Hegemony – A concept from Antonio Gramsci, referring to the dominance of a ruling class through ideology and culture, rather than force.

Human Rights – Universal rights inherent to all individuals, such as freedom, equality, and dignity, often enshrined in international law.

I - L

Ideology – A systematic set of political beliefs guiding individuals and movements, including liberalism, socialism, conservatism, and anarchism.

Justice – The principle of fairness and moral rightness in law, economy, and society. Different theories include Rawls' justice as fairness, Nozick's libertarian justice, and Plato's justice as harmony.

Laissez-Faire – A policy of minimal government intervention in economic affairs, central to classical liberalism and libertarianism.

M

Majoritarianism – The principle that the majority's preferences should guide decision-making in a democracy, sometimes criticized for neglecting minority rights.

Marxism – A socio-political and economic theory developed by Karl Marx and Friedrich Engels, emphasizing class struggle, historical materialism, and the eventual overthrow of capitalism in favor of communism.

Meritocracy – A system in which individuals achieve power and status based on talent, effort, and ability, rather than birth or privilege.

Mixed Economy – An economic system that combines elements of capitalism and socialism, where both the market and government play roles in economic planning and resource distribution.

Monarchy – A system of government where a single ruler (king, queen, or emperor) holds political power, often hereditary and sometimes constitutional.

Multiculturalism – A political and social approach that recognizes and values cultural diversity, promoting integration without assimilation.

Mutualism – A form of anarchist economic theory proposed by

Pierre-Joseph Proudhon, advocating for cooperative exchange and decentralization of economic power.

N

Nation-State – A political entity where a distinct national identity coincides with a sovereign state, often associated with modern nationalism.

Nationalism – A political ideology emphasizing national identity, self-determination, and sovereignty, which can take civic, ethnic, or expansionist forms.

Natural Law – A philosophical concept arguing that certain moral and legal principles exist independently of human legislation and are rooted in human nature. Prominent in Aquinas, Locke, and Rousseau.

Natural Rights – Rights believed to be inherent to human beings by virtue of their existence, rather than granted by governments. John Locke argued for life, liberty, and property as fundamental natural rights.

Negative Liberty – A concept in liberal thought, articulated by Isaiah Berlin, referring to freedom from external constraints imposed by others, particularly the state.

Neoliberalism – A modern economic philosophy advocating free markets, privatization, deregulation, and reduced state intervention, influenced by Friedrich Hayek and Milton Friedman.

Nihilism – A belief in the absence of inherent meaning, purpose, or value, often discussed in political philosophy in relation to radical critiques of morality and authority.

Non-Aggression Principle (NAP) – A fundamental tenet of libertarian thought, stating that the initiation of force against others is unjust, except in self-defense.

O

Oligarchy – A form of governance where power is concentrated in the hands of a small elite, often based on wealth, military control, or political influence.

Oppression – The systematic and unjust exercise of power or authority over marginalized groups, a key concept in feminist, Marxist, and critical race theory.

Overton Window – A concept describing the range of politically acceptable ideas in public discourse at a given time, shifting based on social and political dynamics.

P

Pacifism – A moral and political stance opposing war and violence, sometimes extended to a rejection of all state authority.

Participatory Democracy – A form of democracy that encourages direct citizen involvement in decision-making, beyond just voting for representatives.

Patriotism – A sense of loyalty and devotion to one's nation, distinct from nationalism in that it does not necessarily imply superiority over other nations.

Plutocracy – A government or political system in which wealthy individuals or corporations wield significant power.

Populism – A political movement that claims to represent "the people" against elites, which can take left-wing (economic justice) or right-wing (nationalist, anti-immigrant) forms.

Positive Liberty – The capacity to act with autonomy and self-determination, often requiring social structures that enable personal development (contrast with negative liberty).

Postmodernism – A school of thought that critiques grand narratives, absolute truths, and rigid ideological systems, influencing post-structuralist political theory.

Power – The capacity to influence decisions, behaviors, and institutions, central to political philosophy. Michel Foucault argued that power is diffused through social structures and knowledge systems.

Progressivism – A political philosophy advocating for social reform, economic justice, and government intervention to address inequality.

Proletariat – In Marxist theory, the working class that sells labor to the capitalist class (bourgeoisie) and is central to class struggle.

Property Rights – The legal and philosophical foundation for ownership of resources and goods, central to Locke's theory of natural rights and debated in capitalism vs. socialism.

R

Radicalism – A political stance advocating for fundamental transformation of the existing system, often associated with revolutionary movements.

Realism (Political Realism) – A theory in international relations emphasizing power, self-interest, and competition among states. Prominent figures include Niccolò Machiavelli, Thomas Hobbes, and Hans Morgenthau.

Republicanism – A system of government that emphasizes citizenship, civic virtue, and the public good, rejecting monarchy. Influential in Roman political thought, Machiavelli, and the American Founding Fathers.

Rule of Law – The principle that laws should apply equally to all individuals, preventing arbitrary rule by governments or leaders.

S

Secularism – The separation of religion and government, often debated in relation to pluralism and democracy.

Social Contract – A foundational idea in political philosophy, describing an implicit or explicit agreement among people to form a government. Theories by Hobbes, Locke, and Rousseau differ in scope and justification.

Social Justice – A broad concept advocating for fair distribution of wealth, rights, and opportunities within society. Key figures include John Rawls, Karl Marx, and Nancy Fraser.

Sovereignty – The authority of a state or governing body to rule autonomously, a key issue in debates on nationalism, international law, and globalization.

Statism – The belief that a strong state is necessary to organize society, manage the economy, or enforce order, in contrast with libertarianism and anarchism.

Subsidiarity – A principle in Catholic social teaching and conservative political thought, arguing that decision-making should be decentralized, with smaller institutions handling issues where possible.

T

Theocracy – A government system where religious authority rules directly or strongly influences politics, as in Iran or the Papal States.

Totalitarianism – A political system where the state has absolute control over all aspects of life, with no political opposition. Examples: Nazi Germany, Stalinist USSR, Maoist China.

Tyranny – A government in which power is exercised unjustly or oppressively, often synonymous with dictatorship or autocracy.

U - Z

Utilitarianism – An ethical and political philosophy that advocates for maximizing overall happiness. Jeremy Bentham and John Stuart Mill were its key theorists.

Utopia – A perfect political society envisioned in works like Plato's Republic, Thomas More's Utopia, and Marxist communism.

Welfare State – A government model in which the state actively provides social services, economic security, and public goods to promote social welfare.

Whistleblower – A person who exposes corruption or wrongdoing in government or corporations, often at personal risk.

What is Political Philosophy?

Definition, Scope, and Relationship with Political Science, Ethics, and History

Political philosophy is one of the oldest branches of philosophy, a discipline that concerns itself with the most fundamental questions of governance, justice, power, and human society. At its core, it seeks to answer a set of enduring questions: What is the best form of government? What are the rights and obligations of individuals? What is justice, and how should it be distributed? Who should hold power, and on what basis? These questions, though ancient, are as relevant today as they were in the time of Plato, Aristotle, and Confucius.

To understand political philosophy, we must first distinguish it from political science. While political science is an empirical discipline that studies how political institutions function in practice, political philosophy is normative—it concerns itself with what ought to be rather than merely what is. A political scientist might analyze voting patterns, the behavior of politicians, or the influence of media on elections, but a political philosopher asks: What should a just electoral system look like? A political scientist might examine why certain regimes collapse while others endure, but a political philosopher seeks to determine which form of government is most justified and why.

The Origins of Political Philosophy

The history of political philosophy is the history of human thought about collective life. It is a discipline born out of necessity—whenever humans live together, questions arise about how to distribute power, resolve conflicts, and determine the nature of authority. The first recorded political philosophies emerged in the ancient world, in civilizations as diverse as Greece, China, and India.

Plato, one of the earliest political philosophers, examined the nature of justice in The Republic, envisioning an ideal state ruled by philosopher-kings—those who, by virtue of their wisdom, were best suited to govern. His student, Aristotle, took a more empirical approach, classifying different forms of government and arguing that political systems should be structured to promote human flourishing (eudaimonia). Meanwhile, in China, Confucius emphasized the moral responsibilities of rulers and the importance of virtue in governance, shaping Chinese political thought for millennia.

The questions that preoccupied these early thinkers remain central to political philosophy today. If a government derives its authority from the people, do the people have the right to overthrow it? Should the government prioritize liberty or equality? How do we balance the rights of individuals with the needs of the collective?

The Scope of Political Philosophy

Political philosophy extends far beyond questions of government structure. It touches on fundamental ethical issues, questions of human nature, and the role of institutions in shaping social life. To fully grasp its scope, we must consider its major themes:

The Justification of the State – Why should people accept political authority? Is government a necessary evil, as Hobbes suggested, or is it an instrument for realizing the good life, as Aristotle believed? Theories of the state, such as social contract theory (Hobbes, Locke, Rousseau) and anarchism, provide competing answers.

Power, Authority, and Legitimacy – What distinguishes legitimate authority from mere coercion? Max Weber famously distinguished between traditional, charismatic, and legal-rational authority, offering a framework for understanding why people obey political institutions.

Liberty and Rights – What does it mean to be free? Isaiah Berlin's distinction between negative and positive liberty remains one of the most important conceptual tools in political philosophy. Negative liberty is freedom from external constraints (e.g., government interference), while positive liberty is the ability to achieve one's potential, sometimes requiring state intervention (e.g., education, welfare). The balance between these two forms of liberty is a central issue in political thought.

Justice and Equality – How should wealth, power, and opportunities be distributed in society? Thinkers like John Rawls, who argued for a fair distribution of resources under the "veil of ignorance," and Robert Nozick, who defended property rights and minimal government, offer contrasting perspectives.

Democracy and Its Critics – Democracy is widely regarded as the most legitimate form of government, but it has its detractors. Plato distrusted democracy, seeing it as rule by the ignorant masses. Modern critics point to the influence of money, media, and misinformation in democratic systems.

Political Ideologies – Liberalism, conservatism, socialism, anarchism, and fascism each present different visions of the ideal society. Political philosophy examines their theoretical foundations and their practical implications.

War, Peace, and International Relations – Political philosophy extends beyond the boundaries of the nation-state, addressing questions of war, diplomacy, and global justice. Just War Theory, realism, and cosmopolitanism offer competing frameworks for thinking about international affairs.

Political Philosophy and Ethics

At its heart, political philosophy is deeply intertwined with ethics. The study of ethics concerns what is right and wrong, while political philosophy extends these moral concerns to the public sphere. Consider the question of wealth distribution: Is it morally acceptable for some people to have vast riches while others live in poverty? A political philosopher examines this issue not just in terms of fairness, but in terms of the role of government in rectifying or perpetuating inequalities.

Similarly, debates over individual rights—such as free speech, religious freedom, and the right to privacy—require both ethical and political analysis. Should there be limits on free speech to prevent harm? Is it ever justifiable for the government to prioritize national security over individual privacy? Political philosophy provides the framework for addressing these moral dilemmas in a structured way.

Political Philosophy and History

Political philosophy is not merely an abstract exercise; it is deeply rooted in historical events and real-world struggles. The philosophical ideas of thinkers like John Locke and Montesquieu helped shape the American and French revolutions, while Karl Marx's critique of capitalism influenced socialist movements worldwide.

History provides us with practical case studies of political ideas in action. The failure of communist regimes in the 20th century, for example, offers lessons about the limits of centralized planning and the dangers of totalitarianism. Similarly, the resilience of democratic institutions in some countries—and their collapse in others—raises important questions about what conditions are necessary for political stability.

Moreover, political philosophy often evolves in response to historical developments. The horrors of World War II led to a renewed emphasis on human rights and international law. The rise of digital technology has sparked debates over privacy, surveillance, and the role of artificial intelligence in governance. Just as political philosophy shaped history, history continues to shape political philosophy.

Conclusion: Why Political Philosophy Matters

At a time when political discourse is often polarized, and when governments around the world face crises of legitimacy, political philosophy provides a necessary framework for thoughtful, reasoned debate. It challenges us to question our assumptions, to engage with opposing viewpoints, and to seek a deeper understanding of the principles that underpin our political institutions.

Political philosophy is not just an academic discipline; it is a guide to how we structure our societies, how we make laws, and how we conceive of justice and fairness. It influences everything from the structure of constitutions to the way we think about civil rights, economic policies, and international relations.

Ultimately, the study of political philosophy is an invitation to engage in the grand conversation about human governance that has been ongoing for millennia. It asks us to think critically about power, authority, and justice—not just in an abstract sense, but in the real world, where these questions shape our daily lives.

If we want to be responsible citizens, if we want to build societies that reflect our highest ideals, then we must engage with political philosophy. For in understanding the philosophical foundations of politics, we gain the tools to shape the future—whether through activism, policy-making, or simply the way we vote and participate in civic life.

Political philosophy, then, is not merely an academic exercise. It is a discipline of profound importance, a roadmap for understanding the political world and a means of engaging with it in an informed and thoughtful way.

The State and Its Justification

Theories of the State: Social Contract, Divine Right, Utilitarianism, and Anarchism

The state is one of the most powerful and enduring institutions in human society. It has the authority to enforce laws, collect taxes, regulate behavior, and, in many cases, decide life and death. But what gives the state its legitimacy? Why should individuals obey its laws? And is the state necessary at all? These questions are at the heart of political philosophy and have inspired centuries of debate among philosophers, revolutionaries, and rulers alike.

Throughout history, various justifications for the state have been proposed, each reflecting different assumptions about human nature, morality, and the purpose of government. Four of the most significant theories are the social contract theory, the divine right of kings, utilitarianism, and anarchism. Each offers a distinct perspective on the legitimacy of the state and the obligations of its citizens.

The Social Contract: The State as a Rational Necessity

One of the most influential justifications for the state is social contract theory, which argues that political authority is justified by an implicit agreement among individuals to form a government. This idea, which emerged in early modern Europe, suggests that people consent—either explicitly or tacitly—to give up certain freedoms in exchange for security, order, and the benefits of collective governance.

Hobbes: The Leviathan and the Necessity of Absolute Authority

Thomas Hobbes (1588–1679) provided one of the earliest and most famous versions of social contract theory in his work Leviathan (1651). Hobbes had a pessimistic view of human nature. He believed that in the absence of government—what he called the state of nature—life would be "solitary, poor, nasty, brutish, and short." In this anarchic state, individuals would be in constant conflict, driven by fear, competition, and the instinct for self-preservation.

To escape this chaos, Hobbes argued, people rationally agree to surrender their individual freedoms to a sovereign authority—a Leviathan—which maintains order and prevents the return to the state of nature. The sovereign, whether a monarch or an assembly, must have absolute power to enforce laws and ensure stability. In Hobbes' view, once individuals enter into this contract, they have no right to rebel, no matter how oppressive the ruler may be. The alternative—anarchy—is always worse.

Hobbes' vision of the state is one of necessity rather than morality. The justification for government is not that it is inherently just, but that without it, life would be unbearable.

Locke: Natural Rights and Limited Government

John Locke (1632–1704) offered a more optimistic view in Two Treatises of Government (1689). Like Hobbes, he believed that people leave the state of nature to form a government, but he had a different understanding of both human nature and the purpose of the state.

Locke's state of nature was not as chaotic as Hobbes imagined. He believed that individuals have natural rights—life, liberty, and property—that exist even before government. However, without a formal legal system, these rights are vulnerable to violation. To protect them, people form a government through a social contract.

Unlike Hobbes, Locke argued that this contract is conditional: if a government fails to protect natural rights or becomes tyrannical, the people have the right to revolt. This idea was enormously influential, shaping the American and French revolutions and laying the foundation for modern liberal democracy. In Locke's view, the best form of government is one with limited powers, constrained by laws and accountable to the people.

Rousseau: The General Will and Popular Sovereignty

Jean-Jacques Rousseau (1712–1778), in The Social Contract (1762), took the idea of consent even further. He argued that legitimate government arises not simply from individuals protecting their interests but from their collective will—what he called the general will.

For Rousseau, the state should not be ruled by a king or an elite class but by the people themselves, who should participate directly in governance. He criticized both Hobbes and Locke for their emphasis on individual rights at the expense of community and argued that true freedom comes from submitting to the general will, which represents the common good.

Rousseau's ideas laid the groundwork for modern democracy but also had a darker side: he believed that individuals could be "forced to be free" if they resisted the general will, an idea that later influenced totalitarian ideologies.

The Divine Right of Kings: The State as God's Will

Before the rise of social contract theory, the dominant justification for political authority in medieval and early modern Europe was the divine right of kings. This theory held that monarchs derived their authority directly from God and that their rule was therefore sacred and unquestionable.

Augustine and Aquinas: Theological Justifications for Political Authority

Early Christian thinkers like St. Augustine (354–430) and St. Thomas Aquinas (1225–1274) argued that political authority was part of God's divine order. Augustine saw the state as a necessary institution for restraining human sinfulness, while Aquinas, influenced by Aristotle, viewed government as an instrument for achieving the common good.

The Decline of Divine Right

By the 17th and 18th centuries, however, the divine right of kings was increasingly challenged by thinkers like Locke and Rousseau, as well as by political events like the English Civil War (1642–1651) and the American and French Revolutions. The idea that rulers were accountable only to God was replaced by the idea that governments must be accountable to the people.

Utilitarianism: The State as a Tool for Maximizing Happiness

Utilitarianism, developed by Jeremy Bentham (1748–1832) and John Stuart Mill (1806-1873), offers a different justification for the state. Instead of grounding legitimacy in consent or divine authority, utilitarianism argues that government should exist to maximize the greatest happiness for the greatest number.

Bentham advocated for legal and political reforms based on utility, arguing that laws should be judged by their consequences rather than by tradition or abstract principles. Mill, while largely agreeing with Bentham, introduced concerns about individual liberty, arguing that the state should intervene only when a person's actions harm others (harm principle).

Utilitarianism remains influential in policy-making today, especially in areas like economics, public health, and criminal justice, where cost-benefit analysis plays a key role.

Anarchism: The State as an Unjustifiable Institution

At the opposite end of the spectrum from Hobbes stands anarchism, which rejects the legitimacy of the state altogether. Anarchists argue that all forms of government are inherently oppressive and that people can organize society voluntarily without hierarchical authority.

Proudhon and Bakunin: Against the State

Pierre-Joseph Proudhon (1809–1865), the first to call himself an anarchist, argued that "property is theft" and envisioned a decentralized society based on mutual cooperation. Mikhail Bakunin

(1814–1876) took a more revolutionary stance, advocating for the abolition of the state through direct action.

Modern Anarchism

Anarchist ideas continue to influence social movements, particularly in critiques of capitalism, government surveillance, and police power. While pure anarchism has never been widely implemented, its principles inform libertarian and socialist critiques of centralized authority.

Conclusion: Why the State Exists and Why It Is Debated

The justification of the state remains a central issue in political philosophy. Whether it is seen as a necessary protector (Hobbes), a conditional contract (Locke), an expression of collective will (Rousseau), a tool for maximizing well-being (Bentham and Mill), or an illegitimate institution (anarchists), the debate reflects fundamental tensions between freedom, authority, and justice.

Political philosophy forces us to ask not just whether the state should exist, but what kind of state is just, and how it should serve its people. These are not abstract questions—they shape the real world, from the drafting of constitutions to the justification of revolutions.

Power, Authority, and Legitimacy

The Nature of Political Power, Authority vs. Coercion, and Sources of Legitimacy (Weber, Rousseau, Hobbes)

Few concepts in political philosophy are as fundamental as power, authority, and legitimacy. These ideas are at the core of how societies are structured, how governments operate, and how individuals relate to the state. Power determines who controls resources, makes laws, and enforces social norms. Authority distinguishes between mere force and rightful rule. Legitimacy explains why people obey laws, even when they could, in theory, resist them.

Understanding these concepts allows us to grasp why some political orders persist while others collapse, why some rulers command obedience while others face rebellion, and why the state itself exists in the first place. Thinkers such as Max Weber, Jean-Jacques Rousseau, and Thomas Hobbes have offered influential insights into these themes, shaping the way we understand political life.

The Nature of Political Power

At its simplest, power is the ability to influence or control the behavior of others. In political philosophy, power is not just about physical force—it extends to control over institutions, laws, economic resources, and even the way people think about political reality.

What is Power?

The philosopher Bertrand Russell once defined power as "the ability to produce intended effects." In political terms, this means that a ruler, government, or political movement is powerful if it can shape society according to its will. However, power comes in different forms:

Coercive Power – The ability to force compliance through threats or violence (e.g., a dictator maintaining power through military force).

Economic Power – Control over resources and wealth that can be used to influence behavior (e.g., a corporation funding political campaigns).

Ideological Power – The ability to shape beliefs, culture, and public opinion (e.g., religious institutions or the media influencing social norms).

Institutional Power – Control over legal and political structures that govern society (e.g., the courts, the bureaucracy).

A state or ruler often exercises multiple types of power simultaneously. A government, for example, may enforce laws through coercion (police and military), maintain economic control (taxation and monetary policy), and use ideological power (education systems and propaganda).

Authority vs. Coercion

Power alone does not make a government legitimate. A ruler may have the ability to force people to comply, but this does not mean that people recognize their rule as justified. This distinction between power and rightful rule is captured in the concept of authority.

Authority is power that is viewed as legitimate. It is the difference between a tyrant forcing people to obey through fear and a respected leader whose decisions are willingly accepted by the people.

The German sociologist Max Weber identified three types of authority that explain why people obey rulers:

Traditional Authority – People obey because of longstanding customs and traditions. Monarchies and religious rulers often rely on traditional authority (e.g., the British monarchy).

Charismatic Authority – People follow a leader because of their personal qualities, vision, or leadership (e.g., Mahatma Gandhi, Napoleon, or Martin Luther King Jr.).

Legal-Rational Authority – People obey because of established laws and institutions, not because of a particular leader. Modern democracies are based on legal-rational authority (e.g., the U.S. Constitution).

Weber's framework helps explain why some forms of government persist over time. A dictatorship may rely on coercion, but without legitimacy, it is vulnerable to collapse. A democracy, by contrast, relies on laws and institutions, which remain in place even when individual leaders change.

Coercion Without Authority: The Problem of Illegitimate Rule

A government that relies only on coercion rather than authority is fragile. If a ruler must use constant violence or threats to maintain control, this suggests a lack of legitimacy. History provides many examples of regimes that collapsed because they lacked authority:

The Fall of the Soviet Union (1991) – Despite its immense power, the Soviet state lacked ideological legitimacy by the 1980s, leading to its rapid collapse.

The French Revolution (1789) – The monarchy relied on tradition, but when the public rejected its legitimacy, no amount of force could save it.

When authority is lost, even the strongest governments can be overthrown. This is why political philosophy places such importance on legitimacy—why people obey without needing to be forced.

Legitimacy: Why Do People Obey the State?

Legitimacy is the foundation of stable political rule. A state is legitimate when its people believe it has the right to govern. Different philosophers have proposed different justifications for legitimacy, each offering a unique perspective on why political authority should be obeyed.

Hobbes: Legitimacy Through Fear and Order

Thomas Hobbes (1588–1679) argued in Leviathan that people obey the state because the alternative—anarchy—is worse. In Hobbes' state of nature, life is a violent, chaotic struggle for survival. To escape this, people willingly submit to an absolute ruler who can impose order.

For Hobbes, legitimacy comes not from morality or democracy, but from the state's ability to provide security. If a government fails to do this, it loses its legitimacy, and rebellion becomes justified.

Rousseau: Legitimacy Through the General Will

Jean-Jacques Rousseau (1712–1778) rejected Hobbes' vision of absolute rule. In The Social Contract, he argued that true legitimacy comes from the general will—the collective interests of the people.

Rousseau believed that political authority is only just when it reflects the common good. If a government acts against the general will, the people have the right to overthrow it. This idea was deeply influential in the development of democracy and revolution.

Max Weber: Legitimacy Through Institutions

Weber's theory of legal-rational authority suggests that legitimacy today is mostly grounded in laws and institutions rather than tradition or personal rule. In modern democracies, people obey because they recognize the system—constitutions, laws, elections—as legitimate.

However, Weber also warned that even democracies can lose legitimacy. If legal institutions are seen as corrupt or unfair, people may turn to charismatic leaders or revolutionary movements.

Conclusion: The Fragile Balance of Power, Authority, and Legitimacy

Power, authority, and legitimacy are the foundation of all political systems. Without power, rulers cannot enforce laws. Without authority, power becomes mere coercion. Without legitimacy, authority crumbles, leading to resistance and revolution.

Throughout history, political philosophers have debated what makes a government legitimate:

Hobbes saw legitimacy as the ability to maintain order.

Rousseau saw it as the expression of the people's collective will.

Weber saw it as grounded in tradition, charisma, or legal institutions.

These theories continue to shape modern political thought. Democracies rely on institutions for legitimacy, but when people lose trust in those institutions, populist leaders or authoritarian movements can emerge. Dictatorships, while powerful, remain unstable if they lack legitimacy. Revolutions occur when authority collapses and alternative sources of legitimacy emerge.

The tension between power, authority, and legitimacy is never fully resolved—it is a constant struggle in every political system. Understanding these concepts allows us to critically analyze governments, question the foundations of political obedience, and recognize the conditions that lead to political change.

In the end, the question of legitimacy is not just theoretical—it is deeply practical. It determines whether we obey, resist, or seek to transform the political world we live in.

Justice: The Core of Political Philosophy

Different Conceptions of Justice (Distributive, Procedural, Corrective) and Key Theorists (Plato, Rawls, Nozick)

Few concepts in political philosophy are as enduring, complex, and debated as justice. It is the foundational principle upon which laws, institutions, and societies are built, shaping everything from economic distribution to legal systems and political legitimacy. When we speak of justice, we ask: What does it mean for a society to be just? Who deserves what? How should fairness be determined? These questions lie at the heart of political thought, from Plato in ancient Greece to John Rawls and Robert Nozick in the modern era.

Justice is not a singular concept; rather, it is a constellation of ideas that vary depending on context, ideology, and historical perspective. Broadly speaking, justice can be divided into three primary categories:

Distributive Justice – Concerned with how wealth, power, and resources should be allocated in society.

Procedural Justice – Focuses on the fairness of rules and processes rather than outcomes.

Corrective (or Retributive) Justice – Deals with punishment, reparations, and fairness in rectifying wrongs.

By exploring these categories and the philosophers who shaped them, we can gain a deeper understanding of how justice functions in political thought and why it remains a central concern in governance and social life.

Plato and the Origins of Justice in Political Philosophy

The first major systematic discussion of justice in the Western tradition comes from Plato (428–348 BCE) in The Republic. Plato's concept of justice is deeply tied to his vision of a well-ordered society. He believed that justice is achieved when each individual performs the role for which they are best suited—a principle of specialization and harmony.

The Just Society: Plato's Three Classes

Plato divided society into three distinct classes:

Philosopher-Kings – The ruling class, composed of wise and rational leaders who understand the "Forms" and the ultimate truth.

Guardians (Warriors) – Those who defend the state and maintain order.

Producers (Farmers, Artisans, Merchants) – The economic backbone of society.

Justice, in Plato's view, exists when each class fulfills its designated role and does not interfere with the others. The philosopher-kings govern with wisdom, the warriors maintain security, and the producers provide for society's material needs. This hierarchical but harmonious structure ensures stability and prevents corruption.

For Plato, individual justice mirrors political justice. A just person has a well-ordered soul, where reason rules over spirit and appetite. Just as a city thrives when each class performs its function, an individual is just when their rational faculties govern their desires and emotions.

Plato's vision of justice is deeply anti-egalitarian—he believed that not all individuals are suited to rule, and justice requires a structured social order where each person accepts their role. This perspective stands in contrast to later democratic and liberal theories that emphasize equal opportunity and individual rights.

Distributive Justice: Who Gets What?

Distributive justice concerns the fair allocation of resources, wealth, and opportunities in society. Should goods be distributed equally, based on merit, or according to need? Different theories provide different answers.

John Rawls: Justice as Fairness

Perhaps the most influential modern thinker on distributive justice is John Rawls (1921–2002). In A Theory of Justice (1971), Rawls presents a contractualist approach to justice, arguing that a just society is one that individuals would choose under conditions of fairness.

The Veil of Ignorance

To determine what a just society looks like, Rawls asks us to imagine ourselves behind a veil of ignorance—a thought experiment in which we do not know our race, class, gender, or natural abilities. From this impartial standpoint, he argues, rational individuals would choose two key principles of justice:

The Liberty Principle – Each person should have equal basic rights and liberties, such as freedom of speech, religion, and political participation.

The Difference Principle – Social and economic inequalities are permissible only if they benefit the least advantaged members of society.

This second principle is crucial: Rawls does not advocate strict equality but rather a system where inequalities are justifiable only if they improve the lives of the poor. For example, higher salaries for doctors might be allowed because they provide benefits for society as a whole, but extreme wealth disparities that do not serve the common good would be unjust.

Robert Nozick: Libertarian Critique of Distributive Justice

Rawls' vision of justice was challenged by Robert Nozick (1938–2002) in Anarchy, State, and Utopia (1974). Nozick, a libertarian, rejected the idea that justice requires redistributing wealth for the benefit of society's least advantaged members.

Instead, Nozick argued that justice is based on individual rights and voluntary transactions. He proposed the Entitlement Theory of Justice, which consists of three principles:

Justice in Acquisition – People are entitled to own property if they acquired it fairly (e.g., by mixing their labor with unowned resources).

Justice in Transfer – If property is exchanged voluntarily (e.g., through trade or inheritance), it remains justly held.

Rectification of Injustice – If wealth or property was acquired unjustly (e.g., theft or fraud), there should be a mechanism to correct it.

Nozick rejected patterned distributions of wealth (such as Rawls' Difference Principle), arguing that government intervention in wealth distribution violates individual freedom. If someone becomes wealthy through legitimate means, the state has no right to redistribute that wealth in the name of justice.

His approach aligns with free-market capitalism and critiques welfare-state policies that require taxation for redistribution. According to Nozick, taxation for redistribution is morally equivalent to forced labor because it takes from individuals what they rightfully earned.

Procedural and Corrective Justice: The Fairness of Laws and Punishment

Beyond distributive justice, political philosophers have also debated the fairness of processes and punishments.

Procedural Justice: Fairness in Decision-Making

Procedural justice focuses on fair and impartial processes in legal and political institutions. The idea is that even if outcomes are unequal, as long as the rules are fair, justice is served. Principles of procedural justice include:

Equal application of the law (e.g., no one is above the law).

Transparency in governance (e.g., due process in trials).

Democratic participation (e.g., fair elections).

For example, a fair trial system ensures that all accused persons have legal representation and that evidence is considered objectively, regardless of the verdict.

Corrective Justice: Punishment and Restitution

Corrective justice, also called retributive justice, deals with fair punishment and rectification of wrongs. Philosophers have debated how justice should be enforced when someone violates the rights of others:

Retributive Justice – Punishment should be proportionate to the crime (e.g., "an eye for an eye").

Restorative Justice – Focuses on rehabilitating offenders and compensating victims (e.g., community service, reconciliation programs).

Plato and Kant favored retributive approaches, arguing that justice requires giving individuals what they deserve. By contrast, many modern legal systems incorporate restorative justice, recognizing that rehabilitation may better serve society than mere punishment.

Conclusion: The Ever-Evolving Debate on Justice

The concept of justice remains one of the most contested issues in political philosophy. Plato saw justice as social harmony, Rawls framed it as fairness, and Nozick defended it as liberty and property rights. Whether justice is about equality, fairness of procedures, or just punishment, the debate is far from settled.

What remains clear is that justice is at the core of all political systems—it is the standard by which we judge societies, laws, and leaders. As long as inequality, oppression, and disputes exist, political philosophy will continue to grapple with what justice truly means.

Liberty and Freedom
Negative vs. Positive Liberty, Classical vs. Modern Liberal Perspectives (Berlin, Mill, Rousseau)

Few concepts in political philosophy are as fundamental and yet as contested as liberty and freedom. These ideas lie at the heart of democratic governance, human rights, and political thought more broadly. But what do we mean when we speak of liberty? Is liberty simply the absence of external constraints, or does it also involve the capacity to act in pursuit of one's potential?

Philosophers have long debated these questions, leading to the distinction between negative liberty (freedom from interference) and positive liberty (freedom to achieve self-realization). Thinkers such as John Stuart Mill, Isaiah Berlin, and Jean-Jacques Rousseau have offered competing visions of liberty, shaping modern liberalism, democracy, and even authoritarianism in the process.

By understanding these different perspectives, we can better grasp the political conflicts surrounding liberty today—whether in debates over government regulation, civil rights, or personal autonomy.

The Classical Foundations of Liberty

The philosophical discussion of liberty dates back to ancient Greece and Rome, where thinkers such as Plato, Aristotle, and Cicero explored the relationship between the individual and the state. However, the modern concept of liberty emerged in the 17th and 18th centuries with the rise of liberalism, challenging absolute monarchy and advocating for the rights of individuals against oppressive rulers.

John Locke and the Birth of Classical Liberalism

John Locke (1632–1704) is often considered the "father of liberalism." In Two Treatises of Government (1689), he argued that individuals have natural rights to life, liberty, and property, which governments must protect. For Locke, legitimate government exists by the consent of the governed, and any ruler who violates these rights loses legitimacy.

Locke's view of liberty was largely negative—meaning that freedom consists in the absence of coercion. The role of government is to ensure that individuals can pursue their interests without undue interference. His ideas laid the groundwork for constitutional democracy and influenced the American and French Revolutions.

Negative Liberty: Freedom from Interference

The idea of negative liberty is perhaps most famously articulated by Isaiah Berlin (1909-1997) in his essay Two Concepts of Liberty (1958). Berlin defined negative liberty as the freedom from external constraints—the ability to act without coercion from others, especially the state.

Isaiah Berlin: The Case for Negative Liberty

According to Berlin, a person enjoys negative liberty when they are not hindered by external forces in making choices. This could include:

Freedom of speech – No government censorship.

Economic freedom – The right to buy, sell, and own property.

Personal autonomy – The ability to make decisions about one's own life.

For Berlin, negative liberty is essential in protecting individuals from tyranny. A government that oversteps its role—even with good intentions—risks suppressing individual freedoms. Berlin warned that paternalistic states (governments that interfere for the "good" of citizens) can become oppressive.

Negative liberty has been central to classical liberalism and libertarian thought, influencing free-market advocates such as Friedrich Hayek and Milton Friedman, who argued against government intervention in economic and personal affairs.

John Stuart Mill: Liberty and Harm

Another key defender of negative liberty was John Stuart Mill (1806–1873). In On Liberty (1859), Mill argued that individuals should be free to act however they choose, so long as they do not harm others. This harm principle is a cornerstone of modern liberal thought.

For example:

A person should be free to express any opinion, even if it is offensive.

A person should be free to engage in self-destructive behavior (e.g., drinking, gambling), as long as it does not harm others.

The government should not impose morality (e.g., banning books or restricting lifestyles).

Mill's vision of liberty is not absolute—he supported some government intervention in education and public safety—but he remained deeply skeptical of majority rule and social conformity. He warned that democracy itself can suppress liberty if the majority forces its values on minorities.

Positive Liberty: Freedom to Achieve One's Potential

In contrast to negative liberty, positive liberty is about the ability to act, not just the absence of restrictions. This means having the power or resources to realize one's full potential—for example, through education, economic security, or political participation.

Berlin's Critique of Positive Liberty

Berlin recognized that positive liberty has an attractive side—it focuses on self-mastery, empowerment, and human flourishing. However, he also warned that positive liberty can be dangerous. When states claim they are "liberating" people by forcing them into a collective identity, they often justify authoritarian rule.

For example, totalitarian regimes in the 20th century—such as the Soviet Union—claimed they were ensuring positive liberty by "freeing" people from capitalism, religion, or individualism. This is why Berlin saw negative liberty as a safer and more reliable foundation for political freedom.

Jean-Jacques Rousseau: The General Will and Positive Liberty

One of the most influential advocates of positive liberty was Jean-Jacques Rousseau (1712–1778). In The Social Contract (1762), Rousseau argued that true freedom is not merely freedom from interference but the ability to live according to the "general will"—the collective interest of society.

For Rousseau, people are not truly free when they are ruled by selfish desires or ignorance. Instead, they must participate in direct democracy, shaping laws that reflect the common good. However, he also made the controversial claim that individuals "can be forced to be free"—meaning that if someone resists the general will, they may need to be compelled into compliance.

This idea has been criticized for laying the groundwork for authoritarianism, as it suggests that governments can override individual freedoms in the name of collective welfare. However, Rousseau's focus on civic participation and democracy remains influential.

Classical vs. Modern Liberal Perspectives on Liberty

The debate between negative and positive liberty reflects broader tensions within liberalism.

Classical liberals (e.g., Locke, Mill, Berlin) emphasize negative liberty, limited government, and economic freedom.

Modern liberals (e.g., Rawls, Roosevelt) argue that positive liberty is essential—rights mean little if people lack education, healthcare, or opportunities.

For example:

Classical liberalism supports free markets and opposes excessive state intervention (e.g., Hayek's critique of socialism).

Modern liberalism supports state programs (e.g., public education, welfare, healthcare) as necessary for true freedom.

This debate is reflected in contemporary politics. Libertarians and conservatives tend to favor negative liberty, opposing government regulation and taxation. Progressives and social democrats emphasize positive liberty, arguing that economic and social programs expand meaningful freedom.

Conclusion: The Ongoing Debate on Liberty

Liberty remains one of the most valued and debated principles in political philosophy. While negative liberty protects individuals from oppression, positive liberty seeks to empower people to live fulfilling lives.

The tension between these two forms of liberty shapes political conflicts worldwide—from debates over government intervention in healthcare and education to discussions on free speech vs. hate speech laws.

In the end, both perspectives remind us that freedom is not a single concept but a complex and evolving ideal—one that must constantly be negotiated, defended, and redefined as societies change.

Equality and Rights

The Debate Between Equality of Opportunity vs. Outcome, Natural vs. Legal Rights, and Contemporary Issues (Locke, Rawls, Marx)

Few ideas have shaped political philosophy as profoundly as equality and rights. The struggle for equality has driven revolutions, inspired social movements, and defined political ideologies. But what does it mean for people to be equal? Should society ensure that everyone starts from the same position, or should it also guarantee that everyone achieves similar outcomes? What rights do individuals possess, and are these rights universal or socially constructed?

The debate over equality of opportunity vs. equality of outcome, the distinction between natural rights and legal rights, and the differing perspectives of John Locke, John Rawls, and Karl Marx illuminate the complexities of these issues. These debates continue to shape modern political discourse, influencing policies on education, wealth distribution, social justice, and human rights.

The Meaning of Equality: Opportunity vs. Outcome

At the heart of the discussion on equality lies a fundamental question: Should equality focus on starting conditions or end results?

Equality of Opportunity: A Level Playing Field

Equality of opportunity means that everyone should have a fair chance to succeed, regardless of their background. It does not demand that everyone achieve the same result, but rather that artificial barriers—such as discrimination, privilege, or inherited status—should not determine success.

This idea is central to liberal political thought and is often associated with John Locke and later John Rawls. The principle suggests that if two individuals have the same talents and work ethic, they should have the same chance of success, regardless of their race, gender, or socioeconomic background.

For example, in a society committed to equality of opportunity, education would be freely available to all, ensuring that wealth or class does not determine access to learning. Discrimination based on race or gender would be eliminated from hiring practices, ensuring that jobs go to the most qualified candidates rather than those from privileged backgrounds.

However, critics argue that even with formal equality of opportunity, deep structural inequalities—such as differences in upbringing, social networks, and inherited wealth—mean that real opportunities remain unequal. This concern leads to the argument for equality of outcome.

Equality of Outcome: Addressing Structural Disadvantages

Equality of outcome goes further, suggesting that merely providing equal starting conditions is insufficient if systemic inequalities lead to vastly different results. Instead of ensuring fair competition, this approach aims to reduce disparities in wealth, education, and power, ensuring that actual outcomes are more equal.

This idea is often associated with socialist and Marxist traditions. Karl Marx, for example, argued that economic systems produce class divisions that cannot be overcome merely by equalizing opportunities. For Marx, capitalism inherently leads to the concentration of wealth and power in the hands of a few, necessitating redistributive policies to achieve true equality.

In modern political systems, policies that aim for equality of outcome include:

Progressive taxation (higher tax rates for the wealthy to fund social programs).

Universal healthcare and social welfare to ensure that basic needs are met regardless of income.

Affirmative action programs to correct historical inequalities by giving disadvantaged groups preferential access to education or jobs.

However, critics—especially from libertarian and conservative traditions—argue that equality of outcome undermines individual freedom. They claim that forced redistribution of wealth discourages hard work and innovation, leading to inefficiency and economic stagnation.

The tension between opportunity and outcome remains one of the central debates in modern political philosophy and informs policies around education, taxation, and social justice.

Natural Rights vs. Legal Rights

Another fundamental debate concerns the origin of rights. Do humans possess intrinsic rights that exist independently of governments, or are rights merely legal constructs granted by the state?

Natural Rights: The Legacy of John Locke

The idea of natural rights—also called inalienable rights—originates from natural law theory, which argues that certain rights are inherent to human beings and exist prior to any government or legal system.

John Locke (1632–1704) is the most famous proponent of natural rights. In Two Treatises of Government (1689), Locke argued that all humans possess three fundamental rights:

Life – The right to exist and not be arbitrarily killed.

Liberty – The right to act freely within the limits of not harming others.

Property – The right to own and control possessions obtained through one's labor.

Locke believed that governments exist only to protect these natural rights. If a government violates these rights, citizens have a moral duty to overthrow it—a principle that influenced the American and French Revolutions.

Locke's vision of natural rights is the foundation of liberal democracy and modern human rights discourse. The idea that individuals possess inherent freedoms, regardless of laws or government decrees, underpins documents like the U.S. Declaration of Independence and the United Nations Universal Declaration of Human Rights.

Legal Rights: The Constructivist View

In contrast, some political philosophers—particularly those influenced by legal positivism—argue that rights are not natural but socially constructed. In this view, rights only exist because societies and governments create them through legal and political systems.

For example, the right to vote, healthcare, or education is not something that exists in nature; it is a legal creation that depends on laws and institutions.

Critics of natural rights—such as Jeremy Bentham (1748–1832)—dismissed them as "nonsense upon stilts." Bentham and other utilitarians argued that rights should be based on maximizing overall happiness, rather than abstract notions of what is "natural."

This debate has real-world implications. If rights are natural, then they cannot be denied or taken away by the state. However, if rights are legal constructs, then they can be expanded, modified, or revoked depending on societal changes.

Contemporary Issues in Equality and Rights

Today, debates over equality and rights remain central to political discourse. Some of the most pressing contemporary issues include:

Wealth Inequality – Should governments impose wealth taxes to reduce economic disparities, or does this violate property rights?

Affirmative Action – Should certain groups receive preferential treatment to correct historical discrimination, or does this create reverse discrimination?

Universal Basic Income – Should every citizen receive a guaranteed income to ensure economic security, or would this disincentivize work?

LGBTQ+ Rights – Are these natural human rights that should be recognized globally, or do they depend on cultural and legal recognition?

Healthcare as a Right – Should healthcare be considered a fundamental right, or is it simply a service that individuals must purchase?

Each of these issues reflects deeper philosophical divisions over how we define justice, fairness, and individual freedom.

Conclusion: The Future of Equality and Rights

The debate over equality and rights is not a historical relic—it remains deeply relevant in modern political struggles.

Locke's vision of natural rights and limited government continues to influence classical liberalism and libertarian thought.

Rawls' argument for redistribution to benefit the least advantaged shapes modern social democracy.

Marx's critique of economic inequality fuels socialist and anti-capitalist movements.

The balance between equality of opportunity and equality of outcome, and between natural and legal rights, is unlikely to be resolved definitively. These debates force societies to constantly reassess their values, adapting their legal and economic systems to evolving conceptions of fairness and justice.

As political conflicts over wealth, discrimination, and human rights intensify, one thing remains clear: the fight over equality and rights is far from over.

Ancient Greek Political Philosophy

Plato's Ideal State, Aristotle's Classifications of Government, and Democracy in Athens

Political philosophy, as we understand it today, was largely shaped by the intellectual achievements of Ancient Greece. The period from the 5th to the 4th century BCE was a time of intense philosophical development, as Greek thinkers wrestled with questions about justice, power, and the nature of governance.

Two towering figures—Plato and Aristotle—laid the foundations of Western political thought, offering profound and enduring insights into the structure of the state, the role of rulers, and the nature of citizenship. Their works remain central to political philosophy, influencing thinkers from medieval scholars to modern political theorists.

At the same time, the Athenian experiment with democracy—perhaps the first of its kind in recorded history—provided an early model of popular governance, one that inspired future democratic systems while also attracting significant criticism.

To understand political philosophy's origins, we must explore the ideal state envisioned by Plato, the political classifications of Aristotle, and the reality of democracy in Athens—three interwoven legacies that continue to shape our political world today.

Plato's Ideal State: The Philosopher-King and the Tripartite Society

Plato (427–347 BCE) was one of the first thinkers to systematically examine the nature of justice and the structure of an ideal political order. His vision is most famously articulated in The Republic, a foundational text in political philosophy.

The Central Question: What is Justice?

Plato begins The Republic with a fundamental question: What is justice? Through the dialogues of Socrates and his interlocutors, he dismisses simplistic definitions—such as "justice is the interest of the stronger" (a view offered by Thrasymachus, an early proto-Machiavellian character)—and instead presents a vision of justice as social harmony.

For Plato, justice is achieved when each class in society performs its proper function without interfering with the roles of others. This principle of specialization is central to his ideal state.

The Tripartite Society

Plato's ideal society consists of three rigidly defined classes, each corresponding to a different part of the human soul:

Rulers (Philosopher-Kings) – Representing reason, these individuals are the wisest and most capable of ruling. They are selected through rigorous education and lifelong training.

Guardians (Warriors) – Representing spirit and courage, the guardian class protects the city, maintaining security and order.

Producers (Farmers, Artisans, Merchants) – Representing appetites and desires, this class is responsible for economic production and sustenance.

The Philosopher-King: The Ideal Ruler

Plato believed that only philosophers should rule because they alone possess the wisdom and rational insight to govern justly. In his famous Allegory of the Cave, he describes most people as prisoners of illusion, mistaking shadows for reality. Philosophers, through rigorous training and the pursuit of knowledge, escape this cave and come to understand the true nature of justice and the Good.

Because of their superior knowledge, philosopher-kings rule not for personal gain but for the well-being of the entire state. Unlike democratic rulers, who are subject to public opinion and political rivalries, philosopher-kings are guided solely by reason.

Criticism of Democracy

Plato was deeply skeptical of democracy, particularly the Athenian model, which he blamed for the execution of his mentor, Socrates. He saw democracy as a system ruled by ignorant masses, easily swayed by rhetoric and demagogues. He compared democracy to a ship where the passengers, rather than the skilled captain, determine the course—leading to inevitable disaster.

In Plato's view, democracy degenerates into mob rule, followed by tyranny, as demagogues exploit public passions and fear to seize absolute power. His rejection of democracy would later be challenged by Aristotle, whose view of political systems was more flexible and empirical.

Aristotle's Classifications of Government

Aristotle (384–322 BCE), Plato's most famous student, built upon and criticized his teacher's ideas. While he agreed that politics should aim at the common good, he rejected the rigid idealism of Plato's Republic, preferring an empirical approach based on the study of actual constitutions. His political philosophy is most fully expressed in Politics, where he classifies different forms of government and evaluates their strengths and weaknesses.

The Purpose of the State

Aristotle saw the state (polis) as a natural institution that emerges from human sociality. Unlike Plato, who sought an ideal state detached from real-world examples, Aristotle believed that governments must be based on practical experience and human nature.

The Three Forms of Government (and Their Corruptions)

Aristotle classified governments into three legitimate forms and their degenerate counterparts:

Legitimate Form	Corrupt Form	Definition
Monarchy (rule by one)	Tyranny	A virtuous king rules for the good of all; a tyrant rules for personal gain.
Aristocracy (rule by the best)	Oligarchy	A wise elite governs for the common good; an oligarchy governs for the rich.
Polity (rule by many)	Democracy (mob rule)	A balanced system of shared power; democracy, in its corrupt form, becomes rule by the poor majority over the rich minority.

Aristotle's Preference: The Mixed Government

Unlike Plato, who dismissed democracy outright, Aristotle believed that a "polity"—a mixed government combining elements of democracy and aristocracy—was the most stable system. He advocated for a middle class-based government, believing that extreme wealth or poverty leads to political instability.

Aristotle's classification influenced later political thinkers, including the framers of the U.S. Constitution, who sought a balance of power between the executive (monarchy), Senate (aristocracy), and House of Representatives (democracy).

Democracy in Athens: The First Experiment in Popular Rule

While Plato and Aristotle theorized about politics, Athens practiced democracy—arguably the first recorded attempt at a government "by the people." Athenian democracy, developed in the 5th century BCE, was a direct system where citizens participated personally in decision-making.

Key Features of Athenian Democracy

Direct Participation – Unlike modern representative democracies, Athenian citizens voted directly on laws and policies.

Random Selection – Many public offices were assigned by lot, ensuring that governance was not dominated by elites.

Citizen Assemblies – The Ekklesia (assembly) was open to all male citizens, allowing them to debate and vote on laws.

Limited Citizenship – Women, slaves, and non-citizens were excluded from political participation.

Strengths and Weaknesses

Athenian democracy was remarkably radical for its time, empowering ordinary citizens in an era when most societies were ruled by kings. However, critics (including Plato and Aristotle) saw its flaws:

Demagoguery – Charismatic leaders manipulated public opinion.

Mob Rule – Majority opinion could lead to injustice, as seen in the execution of Socrates.

Exclusionary – Most people (women, slaves) had no political rights.

Despite these flaws, Athenian democracy laid the foundation for modern democratic systems, influencing political thought from the Enlightenment to the present day.

Conclusion: The Legacy of Ancient Greek Political Thought

Plato's vision of a philosopher-king, Aristotle's empirical classification of government, and Athens' experiment with democracy continue to shape modern political thought.

While democracy has become the dominant form of government today, the concerns of Plato and Aristotle remain relevant—how to balance expertise with popular rule, how to prevent tyranny, and how to ensure political stability.

Ancient Greek political philosophy, far from being a relic of the past, still speaks to the most pressing political questions of our time.

Roman and Medieval Political Thought

Cicero's Republicanism, Augustine's City of God, and Aquinas on Law and Justice

The evolution of political thought did not halt with the decline of Ancient Greece. It transitioned into the Roman world, where thinkers such as Cicero articulated a vision of republican government and civic virtue. Following the collapse of the Roman Republic and the rise of empire, Christian theology became a dominant force in political philosophy, with St. Augustine's City of God offering a new framework for understanding political authority in a world increasingly shaped by Christian doctrine. Later, during the Middle Ages, St. Thomas Aquinas synthesized Christian theology with Aristotelian political philosophy, laying the foundations for natural law theory and influencing the development of Western legal traditions.

These three figures—Cicero, Augustine, and Aquinas—represent different stages in the transformation of political philosophy from classical antiquity to the medieval world. Each contributed essential ideas about government, justice, and the role of divine authority, shaping political thought for centuries to come.

Cicero and the Foundations of Roman Republicanism

Marcus Tullius Cicero (106–43 BCE) was one of Rome's greatest statesmen and orators. His political philosophy, deeply influenced by Stoicism and Greek thought, became a defining articulation of Roman republicanism. Unlike Plato and Aristotle, who theorized about the ideal state, Cicero was primarily concerned with practical governance—how to preserve a republic in the face of corruption, ambition, and tyranny.

The Roman Republic and Mixed Government

Cicero defended the Roman Republic, a system of government that blended three different forms:

Monarchy (Consuls) – Two elected officials who served as chief executives.

Aristocracy (Senate) – A body of elite statesmen who advised and shaped policy.

Democracy (Assemblies and Tribunes) – Popular assemblies where citizens could vote on laws and elect officials.

This mixed constitution was designed to balance the stability of monarchy, the wisdom of aristocracy, and the participation of democracy. Cicero admired this system because it prevented any one faction from gaining absolute power—what he feared most was tyranny, whether in the form of a dictator or mob rule.

The Virtuous Statesman and Civic Duty

Cicero's ideal government depended not just on institutions but on virtuous leaders. He believed that moral integrity, wisdom, and dedication to the common good were essential qualities of a ruler. In De Re Publica (On the Republic), he argued that the best rulers are not those who seek personal power but those who act as guardians of the republic.

Cicero's idea of civic virtue—the idea that citizens must actively participate in public life and prioritize the good of the state over personal gain—would later influence Renaissance thinkers and the framers of the U.S. Constitution.

The Fall of the Republic and Cicero's Death

Despite his efforts, Cicero witnessed the collapse of the Roman Republic as Julius Caesar and later Augustus transformed Rome into an empire. Opposing the dictatorship of Mark Antony, Cicero was declared an enemy of the state and executed in 43 BCE. His works, however, survived and influenced generations of political thinkers, including Machiavelli, Montesquieu, and the American Founding

Fathers.

Augustine's City of God: The Christian Transformation of Politics

With the fall of Rome in 476 CE, political philosophy underwent a profound transformation. No longer was politics centered on republics or earthly governance alone—instead, Christian thinkers sought to understand the relationship between divine authority and worldly power.

The most influential figure in this transition was St. Augustine (354–430 CE), whose monumental work The City of God reshaped political thought for the medieval world.

The Two Cities: Earthly vs. Heavenly Rule

In The City of God, Augustine distinguishes between two forms of society:

The City of Man (Earthly City) – Characterized by human pride, sin, and political conflict. Governments in this realm are necessary to restrain human wickedness, but they are always flawed and temporary.

The City of God (Heavenly City) – A divine, spiritual community built on faith, righteousness, and eternal salvation. True justice and peace exist only in this city, not in earthly politics.

Politics as a Necessary Evil

Unlike Greek and Roman philosophers who saw political life as essential to human flourishing, Augustine viewed political authority as a remedy for human sinfulness. He did not reject government outright but saw it as a temporary institution meant to maintain order in a fallen world.

This perspective introduced a theological dimension to political philosophy, shifting the focus from human rationality to divine providence. It also laid the groundwork for later debates about the relationship between church and state.

The Role of Kings and Rulers

Augustine argued that rulers are legitimate only if they govern in accordance with God's will. Unlike Cicero, who emphasized civic virtue and reason, Augustine believed that faith and divine guidance were essential for just rule. This idea influenced medieval kings, who often sought legitimacy from the Church.

Thomas Aquinas: Law, Justice, and Natural Law Theory

As Europe entered the Middle Ages, political thought became dominated by the Church. However, in the 13th century, St. Thomas Aquinas (1225–1274) sought to reconcile Christian theology with Aristotle's political philosophy. His synthesis created one of the most influential theories of law and justice in Western history.

The Four Types of Law

In Summa Theologica, Aquinas developed a hierarchical theory of law, distinguishing four different kinds:

Eternal Law – The divine reason of God, governing the universe.

Natural Law – The part of eternal law that is accessible to human reason, guiding moral behavior.

Human Law – The laws created by governments, which should be based on natural law.

Divine Law – Religious laws revealed through scripture, such as the Ten Commandments.

Natural Law and Political Authority

Aquinas argued that natural law provides the foundation for justice. Human laws are legitimate only if they align with natural law—meaning they must promote the common good and respect human dignity. If a law contradicts natural law (e.g., unjust slavery, tyranny), it is not truly a law and does not need to be obeyed.

This idea—that there is a moral standard higher than human

authority—would later influence the development of human rights and constitutional government.

The Best Form of Government

Aquinas, following Aristotle, believed that the best government is a mixed system that combines monarchy, aristocracy, and democracy. He saw monarchy as the most effective form of rule but warned that kings must govern for the common good, not for personal power.

Unlike Augustine, Aquinas had a more optimistic view of politics, believing that human reason, guided by divine law, could create just political institutions.

Conclusion: The Transition from Classical to Medieval Political Thought

The shift from Roman to medieval political philosophy reflects a broader transformation in how people understood power, justice, and human nature:

Cicero emphasized republicanism, civic virtue, and balanced government, seeking to protect liberty from tyranny.

Augustine introduced a Christian worldview, arguing that political authority is a temporary response to sin and that true justice exists only in the City of God.

Aquinas reconciled Christian theology with Aristotle, laying the foundation for natural law theory and influencing the development of Western legal and political systems.

These ideas did not disappear with the Middle Ages—they shaped Renaissance political thought, the Enlightenment, and modern constitutionalism. The debates about law, authority, and the role of religion in politics that began with these thinkers continue to define our political world today.

Machiavelli and Realpolitik

The Prince and the Birth of Modern Political Strategy

Niccolò Machiavelli (1469–1527) is one of the most controversial and influential figures in the history of political philosophy. His name has become synonymous with cunning, deception, and ruthless pragmatism—so much so that "Machiavellian" is now a term used to describe unscrupulous political maneuvering. However, to reduce Machiavelli's thought to mere deception and cruelty would be a profound misunderstanding.

In his most famous work, The Prince (1513), Machiavelli laid the foundation for what would later be called Realpolitik—a pragmatic, results-oriented approach to political power that prioritizes effectiveness over morality. Departing from the idealistic visions of classical and medieval thinkers, he sought to describe politics as it is, rather than as it should be. In doing so, he shattered traditional notions of virtue in governance, arguing that rulers must be prepared to be ruthless, deceptive, and even cruel if necessary to maintain power and ensure stability.

To fully understand Machiavelli's contributions, we must examine his historical context, the core ideas of The Prince, his influence on modern political strategy, and the birth of Realpolitik.

Historical Context: A Fractured Italy and the Fall of Republican Ideals

Machiavelli was born and lived during the Italian Renaissance, a period of cultural flourishing but also intense political turmoil. Unlike the centralized nation-states emerging in France, England, and Spain, Italy remained a patchwork of warring city-states, constantly threatened by foreign invasions and internal power struggles.

Florence, Machiavelli's home city, was nominally a republic, but it was frequently dominated by the powerful Medici family. In 1494, the Medici were expelled, and Florence briefly experimented with republican rule. Machiavelli rose to prominence as a diplomat and political advisor, serving in the Florentine Republic. However, in 1512, the Medici returned to power, and Machiavelli was arrested, tortured, and exiled from political life.

It was during this period of exile that he wrote The Prince, hoping to regain favor with the Medici rulers. Rather than advocating for the restoration of the republic, he offered a manual for rulers—a guide to acquiring and maintaining power in a dangerous world.

The Prince: Power as It Is, Not as It Should Be

The Prince is unlike any political treatise that came before it. Classical thinkers such as Plato, Aristotle, and Cicero believed that good government should be based on justice, virtue, and the common good. Medieval Christian thinkers, such as Augustine and Aquinas, argued that rulers must be morally righteous and act in accordance with divine law.

Machiavelli rejected these moral frameworks outright. He argued that rulers must not be guided by abstract ideals but by the harsh realities of power. The survival of the state, he contended, is the highest good—even if it requires cruelty, deception, and manipulation.

Virtù vs. Fortuna: The Role of Skill and Luck in Politics

One of the key concepts in The Prince is virtù, which Machiavelli defines not as moral virtue but as political skill, adaptability, and decisiveness. A successful ruler, he argues, must possess strength, intelligence, and a willingness to act ruthlessly when necessary.

However, power is also shaped by fortuna—the unpredictable forces of fate and luck. While no leader can control fortune entirely, Machiavelli insists that those with greater virtù can bend fortune to their will. He famously compares fortune to a raging river that can flood and destroy a state unless the ruler builds strong defenses.

Better to Be Feared Than Loved?

One of the most famous passages in The Prince addresses a fundamental question: Is it better for a ruler to be loved or feared? Machiavelli's answer is unequivocal:

"It is much safer to be feared than loved if one must choose, because men are fickle by nature; they are ungrateful, disloyal, and deceitful."

Love, he argues, is conditional and unreliable—people will abandon a ruler when it suits them. Fear, however, is a stronger motivator. That said, Machiavelli warns that a ruler must avoid being hated, as excessive cruelty can provoke rebellion.

The Ends Justify the Means?

Another infamous claim attributed to Machiavelli is "the ends justify the means." Though he never states this explicitly, The Prince makes it clear that a ruler's actions—no matter how brutal—are justified if they ensure stability and security.

For example:

If lying or breaking treaties helps maintain power, a ruler should do it.

If eliminating political rivals prevents civil war, it is a necessary evil.

If cruelty is needed to establish order, it is preferable to disorder.

This radical pragmatism was shocking to readers at the time, who were accustomed to viewing politics through an ethical or religious lens.

The Birth of Realpolitik: Machiavelli's Influence on Modern Politics

Machiavelli's ideas laid the foundation for Realpolitik, a term that emerged in the 19th century to describe a cold, pragmatic approach to politics based on power rather than ideology or morality. Some of history's most powerful leaders have drawn inspiration—explicitly or implicitly—from The Prince:

Machiavellian Leaders in History

Cardinal Richelieu (France, 17th Century) – The architect of French absolutism, who skillfully used diplomacy, espionage, and manipulation to strengthen the monarchy.

Otto von Bismarck (Germany, 19th Century) – Unified Germany through shrewd diplomacy and military strategy, practicing Realpolitik by balancing alliances and using limited wars.

Napoleon Bonaparte (France, 19th Century) – Master of both warfare and propaganda, Napoleon embodied Machiavelli's belief in power through calculated risk-taking.

Joseph Stalin (Soviet Union, 20th Century) – Ruthlessly eliminated rivals, controlled information, and used fear to maintain power.

Modern Applications of Machiavelli's Thought

Even in democratic societies, Machiavellian strategies shape politics:

Election Campaigns – Politicians craft public images, use deception, and manipulate emotions to win votes.

Diplomacy and Geopolitics – Governments often pursue national interest over ethical considerations (e.g., Cold War strategies, economic sanctions, espionage).

Corporate and Institutional Power – Business leaders and bureaucrats use Machiavellian tactics to consolidate influence, outmaneuver rivals, and control narratives.

Conclusion: The Legacy of Machiavelli

Machiavelli remains one of the most misunderstood yet enduringly relevant political thinkers. While he has been condemned as a cynical advocate of deceit and tyranny, he was, in reality, a realist who sought to understand the mechanics of power.

His work challenged idealistic visions of governance, forcing political theorists and rulers to confront uncomfortable truths about leadership and statecraft. He taught that politics is not a moral playground but a battleground, where power must be won and maintained through intelligence, decisiveness, and sometimes, ruthlessness.

In the modern world, his ideas continue to shape political strategy, diplomacy, and leadership, making The Prince not just a historical text, but an essential guide to understanding power itself.

Hobbes, Locke, and the Social Contract

Leviathan vs. Two Treatises of Government: Contrasting Views on Human Nature and Governance

The story of political philosophy in the modern era cannot be told without an examination of the social contract—one of the most significant and enduring ideas in political thought. It is the idea that political authority does not derive from divine mandate or sheer force but rather from a rational agreement among individuals to form a society. This theory fundamentally redefined governance, shifting power from the hands of kings and placing its justification within human reason and collective will.

Among the thinkers who championed this concept, Thomas Hobbes and John Locke stand as two towering figures, offering competing visions of human nature, political authority, and the purpose of the state. Their respective works, Leviathan (1651) and Two Treatises of Government (1689), present radically different perspectives on why humans create governments, how much power those governments should have, and what rights individuals retain in political society.

To understand their debate is to understand the very foundations of modern political theory, from the absolute power of the state to the birth of liberal democracy, human rights, and revolution.

Thomas Hobbes: The Fearful Origin of Government

Hobbes lived through one of England's most turbulent periods: the English Civil War (1642–1651), which pitted royalists against parliamentary forces, leading to the execution of King Charles I and the temporary abolition of the monarchy. This experience deeply influenced his view of human nature and political authority. In Leviathan, Hobbes does not begin with abstract notions of justice or rights but with a stark and unflinching question: What happens when there is no government at all?

The State of Nature: A World Without Order

Hobbes paints a grim picture of life without government. He calls this the state of nature, a condition in which there is no central authority, no laws, and no structure to regulate human interactions. Without a state, individuals exist in a constant "war of all against all", where life is "solitary, poor, nasty, brutish, and short."

For Hobbes, human beings are not naturally inclined to cooperate. Instead, they are driven by self-preservation, competition, and fear. They may be capable of rational thought, but their rationality leads them to seek power and security at the expense of others. In such a world, trust is impossible, and violence is the natural outcome.

This bleak view of human nature stands in sharp contrast to later thinkers like Locke and Rousseau, who saw human beings as possessing some natural inclination toward morality or cooperation. Hobbes, however, insists that humans do not seek peace out of goodness but out of necessity.

The Social Contract: Surrendering Freedom for Security

Given the chaos of the state of nature, what is the solution?

Hobbes argues that rational individuals will agree to give up their absolute freedom and submit to a sovereign authority in exchange for protection. This is the essence of the social contract: a rational, self-interested decision to escape the horrors of anarchy by creating a powerful state that can impose order.

The ruler—whom Hobbes calls the Leviathan, after the biblical sea monster—must have absolute authority to prevent society from collapsing back into chaos. Whether a monarchy, dictatorship, or even a collective assembly, the Leviathan must possess unchecked power to make and enforce laws, settle disputes, and maintain order.

For Hobbes, there is no right to rebel. Once the contract is made, it is irrevocable. Even if the ruler is cruel or unjust, it is still preferable to the anarchy of the state of nature. The only justification for overthrowing the Leviathan is if it fails entirely to provide security, leaving society once again in a state of war.

The Legacy of Hobbes: Absolute Power and the Birth of the Modern State

Hobbes' vision of government is authoritarian but rational. He does not claim that kings rule by divine right—his justification for absolute power is entirely secular and based on human nature. In this sense, he lays the groundwork for the modern state, where centralized authority is seen as essential for stability.

His ideas influenced later thinkers on both ends of the political spectrum. Absolute monarchs saw in Hobbes a justification for their power, while later social contract theorists—like Locke—built upon his ideas to argue for limited government and individual rights.

John Locke: The Foundations of Liberal Democracy

While Hobbes justified a strong, absolute state, John Locke argued for the exact opposite: a limited government that protects individual freedoms and is accountable to the people. Writing in the aftermath of the Glorious Revolution of 1688, which established a constitutional monarchy in England, Locke's Two Treatises of Government directly challenged Hobbes' pessimistic view of human nature and his justification for absolute rule.

A More Hopeful View of Human Nature

Like Hobbes, Locke begins with the state of nature, but his vision of pre-political life is far less violent. Unlike Hobbes' war of all against all, Locke sees a world where individuals are capable of reason, morality, and cooperation.

He argues that human beings are born with natural rights—life, liberty, and property—that exist prior to government. These rights are not granted by rulers but are intrinsic to human nature, given by God or reason itself.

However, even in Locke's state of nature, conflicts arise—disputes over property, crime, and justice can lead to instability. To resolve these issues, people form governments, but unlike Hobbes, Locke insists that the government must remain limited and serve the people's interests.

The Social Contract: Government as a Trustee of the People

For Locke, individuals enter into a social contract not to surrender all their freedoms but to protect their natural rights. The government is a trustee, holding power only with the consent of the governed.

Unlike Hobbes' Leviathan, Locke's government must be limited and divided, ensuring that no single ruler has unchecked authority. He introduces the idea of separation of powers, later influencing Montesquieu and the framers of the U.S. Constitution.

The Right to Revolution: A Radical Idea

One of Locke's most revolutionary claims is that if a government violates people's natural rights, the people have the right to overthrow it. This directly contradicts Hobbes, who insists that rebellion leads to chaos. Locke, however, argues that tyranny is itself a return to the state of nature—if a ruler behaves as a predator rather than a protector, they forfeit their legitimacy.

This idea became the foundation of modern liberal democracy and directly inspired the American and French Revolutions. When Thomas Jefferson wrote in the Declaration of Independence that all men are "endowed with certain unalienable rights" and that governments derive "their just powers from the consent of the governed," he was echoing Locke's philosophy.

Conclusion: The Clash Between Hobbes and Locke - A Lasting Debate

The contrast between Hobbes and Locke defines one of the central tensions in political philosophy:

Hobbes prioritizes security over freedom, arguing that strong authority is necessary to prevent chaos.

Locke prioritizes liberty, arguing that government must be restrained to protect individual rights.

Their ideas continue to shape debates about the role of the state, the limits of government power, and the balance between security and freedom. Should we, in times of crisis, expand government power for the sake of security? Or should we always prioritize individual liberty, even at the risk of disorder?

These are the questions that Hobbes and Locke force us to confront, and they remain as relevant today as they were in the 17th century. Their debate is not just historical—it is the philosophical foundation of modern democracy and authoritarianism alike.

Rousseau and the General Will

Democracy, Collective Sovereignty, and the Critique of Civilization

Few thinkers in the history of political philosophy have been as radical, as provocative, or as misunderstood as Jean-Jacques Rousseau (1712–1778). A man who stood at the crossroads between the Enlightenment and the Romantic era, Rousseau was both a champion of democracy and a harsh critic of civilization. He was a thinker who inspired both the French Revolution and its subsequent descent into authoritarianism. His concept of the general will, the heart of his political theory, has been read as both the foundation of popular sovereignty and a justification for oppressive collectivism.

To engage with Rousseau is to enter a world where the fundamental questions of political philosophy—freedom, equality, power, and the legitimacy of rule—are reimagined in ways that continue to shape modern politics. His work rejected monarchy, challenged the very nature of social hierarchies, and sought to redefine democracy in a way that remains controversial to this day.

The State of Nature: A Different Vision of Humanity

To understand Rousseau's political thought, one must begin with his radical departure from earlier social contract theorists, particularly Thomas Hobbes and John Locke. Like them, Rousseau asked: What was humanity like before the formation of society? But his answer was entirely different.

Hobbes had argued that life without government was "solitary, poor, nasty, brutish, and short," a chaotic state of constant war where humans sought power at each other's expense. Locke had presented a more optimistic view, where individuals were capable of reason and morality even in the absence of government. Rousseau, however, dismissed both as projecting their own era's corrupt social relations onto the distant past.

For Rousseau, the original human—the human in the true "state of nature"—was neither brutal nor rational in the way his predecessors described. Instead, he was a solitary, peaceful, and simple creature. In his famous Discourse on the Origin and Foundations of Inequality Among Men (1755), Rousseau imagined an early human who was self-sufficient, motivated by basic needs, and possessing a deep capacity for compassion. This was not the selfish brute of Hobbes or the calculating property-owner of Locke, but rather a being guided by instinct, immediate desires, and a natural form of pity for others.

Then came civilization—and with it, inequality, competition, greed, and oppression.

Rousseau's claim was astonishing in its subversion of Enlightenment ideals. Most thinkers of his era saw civilization as the triumph of reason and progress over primitive ignorance. Rousseau saw the opposite: civilization was the corruption of human beings, the process by which they became enslaved to vanity, competition, and artificial desires.

And yet, despite this critique, Rousseau was not an anarchist. Unlike later Romantics who would idealize the "noble savage", he did not advocate a return to primitive life. Instead, he sought a new kind of political order—one that could restore the lost freedom of humanity without plunging into barbarism. That order would be based on the general will.

The Social Contract and the General Will

Rousseau's most influential political work, The Social Contract (1762), begins with one of the most famous sentences in political philosophy:

"Man is born free, and everywhere he is in chains."

Here, Rousseau is not merely speaking of literal slavery or despotism. He is talking about the entire structure of modern society, which forces individuals into artificial hierarchies, economic dependence, and subjugation to rulers who do not represent their interests.

But unlike earlier social contract theorists, who argued that individuals trade some freedoms for the security of government, Rousseau was not willing to accept any loss of real freedom. Instead, he proposed a radical new idea: that a society could be built in which people remain as free as they were in the state of nature, while still benefiting from collective governance. The key to this vision was the general will.

What Is the General Will?

The general will is perhaps the most debated concept in Rousseau's philosophy. At its core, it represents the collective interest of the people, the shared vision of what is best for society as a whole. Unlike the will of all, which simply sums up individual desires, the general will transcends individual interests and expresses the common good.

A political society governed by the general will does not simply reflect what the majority wants at any given moment. It represents the rational and moral interest of the people as a collective, even if individuals might not always recognize it themselves.

For Rousseau, true freedom is found not in individualism but in participation in a collective political order that represents the real interests of its members. People obey laws not because they are forced to, but because those laws reflect their own deeper interests as members of the community.

Direct Democracy: Collective Sovereignty

This leads to Rousseau's vision of democracy, which is strikingly different from the representative systems of today. Rousseau argued that true political freedom requires direct participation—a form of democracy in which citizens themselves deliberate and decide laws, rather than entrusting representatives to govern on their behalf.

In Rousseau's model, sovereignty can never be delegated. If a people elect representatives to make decisions for them, they are not truly free. Instead, each citizen must be an active participant in shaping the laws that govern them.

This is an incredibly demanding model of politics, one that perhaps only small city-states could realistically sustain. But Rousseau believed that any government claiming to represent the people must be constantly checked to ensure that it aligns with the general will, rather than the private interests of the powerful.

The Danger of Forced Freedom: Rousseau's Most Controversial Idea

One of Rousseau's most troubling claims is his assertion that individuals who resist the general will "can be forced to be free."

This phrase has led to accusations that Rousseau was an authoritarian in disguise, a thinker whose vision of democracy contains the seeds of tyranny. And indeed, later revolutionaries—particularly the radical Jacobins of the French Revolution—invoked Rousseau's ideas to justify political purges and the suppression of dissent.

Yet Rousseau himself was no advocate of dictatorship. His claim about "forcing freedom" comes from the belief that people sometimes do not recognize their own true interests. If individuals act out of selfishness rather than in pursuit of the general good, the state must sometimes compel obedience.

This is an incredibly dangerous argument—one that, in the wrong hands, can justify political oppression in the name of an abstract collective good. But Rousseau's deeper message remains relevant: freedom is not merely the absence of constraints but the ability to participate meaningfully in a society that expresses one's true interests.

Conclusion: Rousseau's Enduring Influence and Controversy

Rousseau's ideas inspired revolutions, shaped democratic theory, and raised deep ethical questions that remain unresolved. His emphasis on popular sovereignty and direct democracy influenced the French and American Revolutions, the development of socialist and communal political movements, and even the concept of participatory democracy in modern governance.

Yet his notion of the general will continues to provoke debate. Is it a noble vision of a just society, or a dangerous abstraction that enables political coercion? Can modern democracies truly balance collective sovereignty with individual liberty?

Rousseau challenges us to rethink the relationship between freedom, equality, and political participation. His work remains as urgent and unsettling today as it was in his time. And whether one sees him as a champion of democracy or a philosopher of totalitarian temptation, his ideas cannot be ignored.

Liberalism: Classical vs. Modern

From Adam Smith to John Stuart Mill and Contemporary Liberal Thought

Few political philosophies have shaped the modern world as profoundly as liberalism. It is the foundation of constitutional democracy, free-market economics, and the very notion of individual rights. Yet, liberalism is not a single, unified doctrine. It has evolved over centuries, responding to changing social, economic, and political realities.

At its core, liberalism is a philosophy of freedom, but what that freedom entails has been the subject of intense debate. Is it simply the right to be left alone by the state, free to pursue one's own interests? Or does true freedom require social and economic conditions that allow all individuals to fully participate in society? These questions define the historical divide between classical and modern liberalism.

The story of liberalism is one of tension—between economic freedom and social justice, between individual rights and collective responsibility, between the free market and the role of the state. To understand this dynamic, we must examine the origins of liberal thought in the work of Adam Smith, the moral and political refinements of John Stuart Mill, and the transformation of liberalism in the contemporary era.

The Birth of Classical Liberalism: Adam Smith and the Free Market

The roots of classical liberalism can be traced to the 17th and 18th centuries, when European philosophers began challenging the authority of absolute monarchs, mercantilist economics, and religious dogma. The emerging liberal vision called for limited government, free markets, and individual liberty, seeking to replace rigid social hierarchies with meritocracy and personal choice.

One of the most influential figures in this tradition was Adam Smith (1723-1790), the Scottish philosopher and economist whose seminal work, The Wealth of Nations (1776), laid the intellectual groundwork for free-market capitalism.

Economic Freedom and the Invisible Hand

Smith's central argument was radical for its time: economic prosperity does not require state control. In fact, governments should step back and allow individuals to pursue their own interests in the marketplace. He introduced the concept of the "invisible hand"—the idea that individuals, by seeking their own gain, indirectly contribute to the overall well-being of society.

This was a revolutionary break from the dominant mercantilist policies of the era, which saw the economy as something that had to be carefully managed by the state. Smith argued that competition, voluntary exchange, and the division of labor would create a more prosperous society than any system of government intervention.

Yet, Smith was not a laissez-faire extremist. He recognized that markets could fail, that monopolies could arise, and that governments had a duty to provide basic public goods such as education, infrastructure, and legal protection. But his core belief remained: economic liberty was the key to prosperity and human flourishing.

Classical Liberalism and Political Thought

Beyond economics, classical liberals championed individual rights, private property, and constitutional government. Thinkers such as John Locke, Montesquieu, and Thomas Jefferson argued that governments should exist only to protect natural rights, not to control people's lives. Classical liberals were deeply skeptical of government power, fearing that it would inevitably lead to tyranny.

This skepticism led to the promotion of limited government, where the state's role was minimal, focused primarily on protecting life, liberty, and property. The U.S. Declaration of Independence and the Constitution were directly shaped by these principles, emphasizing free speech, the rule of law, and representative democracy.

But as society changed, so too did the liberal vision. By the 19th century, industrialization, urbanization, and growing economic inequality forced liberals to reconsider the meaning of freedom.

John Stuart Mill and the Evolution of Liberal Thought

If Adam Smith represents the birth of economic liberalism, then John Stuart Mill (1806-1873) represents its transformation into a broader, more nuanced philosophy. Mill was a defender of individual liberty, but unlike earlier liberals, he recognized that economic freedom alone was not enough—social and political freedoms mattered just as much.

On Liberty: The Harm Principle and Individual Rights

Mill's most famous work, On Liberty (1859), introduced one of the most enduring principles in liberal philosophy:

"The only freedom which deserves the name is that of pursuing our own good in our own way, so long as we do not attempt to deprive others of theirs, or impede their efforts to obtain it."

This is what he called the harm principle—the idea that individuals should be free to act however they choose, so long as their actions do not harm others. This principle became the cornerstone of modern liberal democracy, supporting freedom of speech, freedom of religion, and personal autonomy.

Mill's defense of liberty was not just about protecting individuals from the state; he was also deeply concerned about social pressure and conformity. He feared that majority rule could become a form of tyranny, where public opinion suppresses individuality. This insight remains relevant in contemporary debates about cancel culture, political correctness, and free speech in the digital age.

The Role of the State: A Shift Toward Social Liberalism

While Mill remained committed to free markets, he recognized that pure laissez-faire economics could lead to deep inequalities. Unlike earlier classical liberals, Mill saw a role for government intervention in education, poverty relief, and worker protections.

This marked a shift toward modern liberalism, a form of liberal thought that still values individual freedom but accepts that some level of state action is necessary to create fair opportunities for all.

Modern Liberalism: Expanding Freedom in a Complex World

By the late 19th and early 20th centuries, liberalism split into two competing visions. Classical liberals continued to defend free markets and minimal government, while modern liberals began arguing that real freedom requires more than just the absence of state interference.

Key Features of Modern Liberalism

Modern liberals—exemplified by thinkers such as John Maynard Keynes, Franklin D. Roosevelt, and John Rawls—believed that governments must:

Regulate markets to prevent economic crises, monopolies, and worker exploitation.

Provide public education, healthcare, and welfare to ensure equal opportunity.

Expand civil rights to protect marginalized groups.

This shift in liberalism led to the rise of the welfare state, seen in policies such as Roosevelt's New Deal, Britain's National Health Service, and social democracy in Scandinavia. These policies sought to balance economic growth with social justice, creating a hybrid of capitalism and government intervention.

The Classical Liberal vs. Modern Liberal Divide

Today, the divide between classical and modern liberalism is one of the most contentious in political philosophy.

Classical liberals (libertarians and free-market conservatives) argue that government should be as small as possible, fearing that modern liberal policies lead to excessive taxation, bureaucracy, and reduced economic growth.

Modern liberals (progressives and social democrats) argue that true freedom means access to education, healthcare, and economic security, and that markets alone cannot deliver these essentials.

This debate shapes political conflicts across the world, from debates over taxation and healthcare to disagreements about the role of government in personal lives.

Conclusion: Liberalism in the 21st Century

Liberalism remains the dominant political philosophy of the modern world, but it is also a philosophy in crisis. Rising inequality, corporate power, and global challenges like climate change have reignited debates about the limits of free markets. Meanwhile, liberal democracy itself faces growing threats from authoritarian populism and nationalist movements.

The fundamental question remains: what does it mean to be free? Does freedom mean the right to be left alone by the state, or does it require active government intervention to ensure real opportunities for all?

The tension between classical and modern liberalism is not just an academic debate—it is the defining political struggle of our time.

Marxism and Critiques of Capitalism

Historical Materialism, Class Struggle, and the Communist Manifesto

No political philosophy has been as fiercely debated, as passionately defended, or as vehemently opposed as Marxism. For some, it is the key to understanding history and liberating humanity from oppression; for others, it is a dangerous ideology that leads to authoritarianism and economic collapse. Either way, it cannot be ignored. Marxism is not merely a theory of economics or government—it is a comprehensive framework for understanding human history, power, and the structure of society itself.

At the heart of Marxist thought lies a profound critique of capitalism—a critique that remains deeply relevant in today's world of corporate dominance, wealth inequality, and economic instability. But Marxism is not just about tearing down capitalism; it also envisions an alternative: a classless, stateless society based on collective ownership of the means of production.

To grasp the power of Marxist theory, we must explore historical materialism, class struggle, and the ideas set forth in The Communist Manifesto (1848), the most influential revolutionary text of modern times.

Historical Materialism: The Marxist Lens on History

Karl Marx (1818–1883) and his lifelong collaborator Friedrich Engels (1820–1895) did not see themselves as utopian dreamers. Unlike idealists who built political theories around abstract principles, Marx and Engels insisted that politics, economics, and ideology were all grounded in material conditions.

This is the foundation of historical materialism, a theory that seeks to explain human history not through ideas, culture, or morality, but through the way societies organize production and distribute resources.

Marx argues that the driving force of history is not great leaders or philosophical ideas, but economic systems and class relations. Every society, from ancient civilizations to feudal Europe to industrial capitalism, has been shaped by its mode of production—the way wealth is created and who controls that wealth.

The Structure of Society: Base and Superstructure

In Marxist analysis, society consists of two fundamental layers:

The Base – The economic system of a society, including the means of production (factories, land, resources) and the relations of production (who owns what, who works for whom).

The Superstructure – The institutions, laws, culture, religion, and political systems that emerge from and serve the interests of the ruling economic class.

The base shapes the superstructure. In a capitalist society, for example, the legal system, media, and educational institutions reinforce the interests of the capitalist class—convincing workers that the system is natural, just, and inevitable.

This radical view suggests that ideologies are not neutral; they are tools of power. Religion, nationalism, and even philosophy itself, Marx argued, often serve to justify existing class structures rather than challenge them.

Class Struggle: The Engine of History

For Marx, history is a history of class struggles. From slave societies to feudalism to capitalism, human societies have always been divided into oppressors and oppressed. Each economic system creates distinct classes that are in conflict over the distribution of wealth and power.

Feudalism to Capitalism: The Rise of the Bourgeoisie

In feudal Europe, the dominant classes were:

The Aristocracy (landowning nobles) – Who controlled land and extracted wealth from...

The Peasantry – Who worked the land and were largely bound to it by tradition and coercion.

With the rise of industrial capitalism in the 18th and 19th centuries, feudalism gave way to a new system, in which wealth was no longer derived from land but from industry and trade. This shift created two new primary classes:

The Bourgeoisie – The owners of capital, factories, and businesses.

The Proletariat – The working class, who owned nothing but their labor and were forced to sell it to survive.

Unlike feudalism, where class divisions were upheld by hereditary tradition, capitalism appeared to offer freedom. Workers were no longer legally bound to landowners, and in theory, they could sell their labor to the highest bidder. But Marx saw through this illusion.

Capitalism and Exploitation

Marx argued that capitalism was just a new form of domination, more sophisticated but no less oppressive than feudalism. The bourgeoisie exploit the proletariat by paying them less than the value of what they produce. The difference—the surplus value—is pocketed by the capitalist as profit.

In other words, workers create all economic value, but capitalists take the rewards. Marx saw this as a fundamental contradiction in capitalism, one that would eventually lead to its downfall.

The Communist Manifesto: A Call to Revolution

In 1848, as revolutions swept across Europe, Marx and Engels published The Communist Manifesto, a short but incendiary text that remains one of the most influential political documents in history.

"A Spectre is Haunting Europe"

The manifesto opens with a bold proclamation:

"A spectre is haunting Europe—the spectre of communism."

Marx and Engels argue that capitalist societies are doomed. The very success of capitalism, which has revolutionized production and created global markets, will eventually undermine itself. Capitalism produces both immense wealth and deep poverty, concentrating power in fewer and fewer hands while leaving the majority struggling to survive.

This, they argue, is unsustainable. Sooner or later, the workers will rise up, overthrow the bourgeoisie, and establish a new socialist society.

The Abolition of Private Property

Perhaps the most controversial demand in the manifesto is the call to abolish private property. Marx and Engels clarify that they do not mean personal possessions—people would still own homes, clothes, and personal goods. What they mean is the abolition of private ownership of the means of production—factories, land, and resources—so that they can be controlled collectively.

The manifesto lays out a series of revolutionary goals, including:

Progressive taxation

Abolition of inheritance rights

State-controlled education

Public ownership of key industries

The Future: From Socialism to Communism

After the proletariat seizes power, they must establish a dictatorship of the proletariat, where the state works on behalf of the workers rather than the capitalists. Over time, as class distinctions disappear and people learn to govern themselves collectively, the state itself will "wither away," leading to true communism—a society without classes, without exploitation, and without government coercion.

The Legacy and Criticism of Marxism

Marxism has inspired revolutions and shaped the modern world, from the Soviet Union and Maoist China to social democracies in Europe. It has also been severely criticized, both by opponents of socialism and by those who argue that Marx failed to anticipate the adaptability of capitalism.

Critics argue that Marx underestimated the ability of capitalism to reform itself, as seen in the rise of labor rights, social welfare programs, and democratic governance. Others claim that communist revolutions have often led to authoritarianism rather than liberation, as seen in the history of the USSR.

Yet, even in capitalist societies, Marx's critique remains relevant. The persistence of wealth inequality, corporate power, and economic crises continues to fuel debates about whether capitalism is truly sustainable.

Conclusion: The Enduring Relevance of Marxist Thought

Whether one sees Marxism as a road to freedom or a dangerous ideology, it cannot be ignored. Marx's analysis of capitalism, class struggle, and economic power remains one of the most compelling critiques of modern society.

The questions he raised—Who controls wealth? Who benefits from economic growth? What role should the state play in redistribution?—are as urgent today as they were in the 19th century.

Marx's revolution may not have happened as he predicted, but his challenge to capitalism still defines the political struggles of the modern world.

Utilitarianism and Political Decision-Making
Bentham, Mill, and the Greatest Happiness Principle in Law and Policy

Few philosophical traditions have had as direct and measurable an impact on political decision-making as utilitarianism. While many political theories wrestle with abstract ideals—justice, liberty, equality—utilitarianism asks a far more pragmatic question: What policies produce the best overall outcomes for the greatest number of people?

It is a philosophy that sees ethics and governance as a science, a system of maximizing well-being and minimizing suffering. Utilitarianism, particularly as formulated by Jeremy Bentham (1748–1832) and John Stuart Mill (1806–1873), has left a profound mark on legal systems, public policy, and economic theory. It has shaped everything from criminal justice reform to cost-benefit analysis in government planning.

Yet, despite its widespread influence, utilitarianism is not without its philosophical and ethical challenges. Can morality really be reduced to calculations of happiness? Should the rights of the few ever be sacrificed for the well-being of the many? These tensions lie at the heart of both utilitarian political thought and the real-world policies that have attempted to implement it.

The Birth of Utilitarianism: Jeremy Bentham and the Calculus of Pleasure and Pain

Jeremy Bentham, an English philosopher and social reformer, is widely regarded as the father of utilitarianism. He was a radical thinker, deeply critical of the legal and political systems of his time, which were still grounded in tradition, privilege, and religious dogma. Bentham sought to replace these outdated ideas with a scientific, rational approach to ethics and law—one that could be tested, measured, and applied universally.

His solution was the principle of utility—the idea that actions and policies should be judged solely by their consequences, specifically their ability to produce pleasure and reduce pain.

The Greatest Happiness Principle

Bentham's fundamental maxim can be summed up in a single phrase:

"The greatest happiness of the greatest number is the measure of right and wrong."

This principle, sometimes called the greatest happiness principle, argues that:

All human actions are motivated by pleasure and pain—these are the fundamental forces of human behavior.

Governments and laws should aim to maximize overall happiness and minimize suffering.

Ethical and political decisions should be judged by their outcomes, not by intentions, traditions, or moral absolutes.

To Bentham, concepts like natural rights, divine law, or inherited privilege were meaningless. A good policy was not one that followed religious commandments or historical precedent but one that resulted in the best overall consequences for society.

The Utility Calculus: Can Morality Be Measured?

Bentham even attempted to quantify morality through what he called the felicific calculus—a system for measuring pleasure and pain based on factors such as:

Intensity – How strong is the pleasure or pain?

Duration – How long does it last?

Certainty – How likely is it to occur?

Extent – How many people are affected?

This mathematical approach to morality was groundbreaking. It suggested that political decision-making should not be based on vague notions of justice or virtue but on empirical evidence and logical reasoning. In other words, governments should function like moral accountants, adding up benefits and harms to determine the best possible policies.

Yet, as Bentham's critics pointed out, can happiness really be measured? And even if it can, should we always act in ways that produce the most happiness, even if it means sacrificing individual rights?

This is where John Stuart Mill enters the debate.

John Stuart Mill: Refining Utilitarianism and Defending Liberty

John Stuart Mill was both a disciple and a critic of Bentham. He accepted the greatest happiness principle but believed that Bentham's version was too simplistic, too focused on quantity over quality.

Mill worried that Bentham's utilitarianism reduced human life to a mere calculus of pleasure and pain, failing to recognize the richness and complexity of human happiness. He sought to refine the theory to make it compatible with individual liberty, dignity, and higher forms of human fulfillment.

Higher and Lower Pleasures: Not All Happiness is Equal

One of Mill's most famous contributions was his distinction between higher and lower pleasures. Bentham had treated all forms of pleasure as equal—eating a fine meal, listening to music, or indulging in hedonistic pleasure were all simply sources of happiness.

Mill, however, argued that some pleasures are intrinsically superior to others. Intellectual and artistic fulfillment, moral virtues, and deep relationships contribute to a richer, more meaningful life than simple sensory pleasures.

This led to his famous assertion:

"It is better to be a human being dissatisfied than a pig satisfied; better to be Socrates dissatisfied than a fool satisfied."

For Mill, utilitarianism was not just about maximizing happiness in the simplest sense; it was about cultivating the best possible society, one that encourages human flourishing, knowledge, and freedom.

Utilitarianism and Liberty: The Role of the State

While Bentham had been largely indifferent to individual rights, seeing them as abstract nonsense, Mill sought to reconcile utilitarianism with personal liberty. In On Liberty (1859), he argued that a truly free society is one that protects individual choice, diversity, and free expression—not just for their own sake, but because they lead to greater well-being in the long run.

He introduced the harm principle, stating that:

"The only purpose for which power can be rightfully exercised over any member of a civilized community, against his will, is to prevent harm to others."

This principle became the foundation for modern liberal democracy, free speech protections, and limited government. Mill's utilitarianism thus took on a more humanistic, rights-based approach, balancing social welfare with individual freedoms.

Utilitarianism in Law and Policy: A Legacy of Reform

While utilitarianism is often debated as a philosophical theory, its influence on real-world political decision-making is undeniable. Bentham and Mill directly inspired progressive legal and social reforms, many of which remain central to modern governance.

Legal Reforms: Punishment and Crime

Bentham was an early advocate for criminal justice reform, arguing that punishments should be based not on revenge but on their effectiveness in reducing crime. He opposed harsh, arbitrary punishments and believed that penalties should be proportional, consistent, and focused on rehabilitation.

This utilitarian approach continues to shape criminal justice policies, from sentencing guidelines to debates about the death penalty.

Economic and Social Policy: The Welfare State

Modern welfare policies—from public healthcare to progressive taxation—are often justified using utilitarian reasoning. Governments frequently rely on cost-benefit analysis, a direct descendant of Bentham's utility calculus, to determine policies that maximize public well-being.

For example:

Public healthcare is justified on the grounds that it improves overall happiness and economic productivity.

Taxation and redistribution aim to reduce suffering and increase well-being for the majority.

Education policies are based on maximizing social mobility and long-term happiness.

Ethical Dilemmas: The Limits of Utilitarianism

Yet utilitarianism is not without its moral challenges. The biggest critique remains: Does the end always justify the means?

Would it be justifiable to sacrifice one innocent person if it meant saving a thousand?

Should we violate individual rights if doing so increases overall happiness?

Can happiness truly be measured, or is it too subjective?

These questions continue to fuel debate about the role of utilitarianism in politics, law, and ethics.

Conclusion: Utilitarianism's Enduring Influence

Despite its challenges, utilitarianism remains one of the most influential and pragmatic frameworks for political decision-making. Its emphasis on evidence-based policy, social progress, and rational governance has shaped modern legal systems, economic policy, and human rights.

Yet the core tension of utilitarianism persists: Can we balance the greatest good for the greatest number with the protection of individual rights and freedoms? This remains one of the defining moral and political questions of our time.

Libertarianism and Minimal Government

Nozick, Hayek, and the Arguments for a Free-Market State

Among the most enduring and radical political philosophies of modern times, libertarianism presents a vision of society where individual liberty reigns supreme, government is strictly limited, and free markets serve as the primary engine of prosperity and justice. It is a philosophy that resists the creeping expansion of state control, viewing government as a necessary evil at best and a dangerous oppressor at worst.

In its purest form, libertarianism advocates for a "night-watchman state"—a government so minimal that it exists only to protect individuals from force, fraud, and coercion. Beyond that, libertarians argue, people should be free to engage in voluntary exchanges, pursue their own interests, and structure their lives without interference from bureaucrats or politicians.

This philosophy has been championed by thinkers such as Robert Nozick, who argued for a radically limited state based on property rights, and Friedrich Hayek, who warned of the dangers of government overreach in economic planning. Their ideas have shaped economic policies, legal debates, and resistance to state intervention across the world, influencing everything from taxation policies to debates over personal freedoms and market regulations.

To understand libertarianism, we must explore its philosophical foundations, its arguments for free markets, and its critique of government intervention.

The Foundations of Libertarianism: Individual Rights and the Limits of the State

Libertarianism is fundamentally a philosophy of individual autonomy. It begins with the belief that people have natural rights—rights that exist independently of government or society. These rights are typically seen as negative rights, meaning they are freedom from interference rather than entitlements to certain goods or services.

For libertarians, the role of government should be strictly limited to protecting these rights, not providing welfare, regulating markets, or redistributing wealth. The state should act only as a protector of property, enforcer of contracts, and defender against external threats.

Libertarians argue that whenever governments go beyond these core functions, they violate individual liberty and create inefficiencies that ultimately harm society.

Robert Nozick: The Minimal State and the Argument Against Redistribution

One of the most famous libertarian philosophers of the 20th century, Robert Nozick (1938–2002), developed a robust defense of minimal government in his landmark work, Anarchy, State, and Utopia (1974). Written as a response to John Rawls' theory of justice, Nozick's work is a full-throated rejection of government redistribution and state intervention in economic affairs.

Nozick's argument begins with a fundamental question: What justifies the state's existence at all? Unlike anarchists, Nozick does believe that some government is necessary—but only in its most minimal form.

For Nozick, the only legitimate function of government is to prevent force, fraud, and theft. Beyond that, any government action—including taxation for social programs—is morally illegitimate because it violates individuals' rights.

His famous analogy compares taxation to forced labor:

"Taxation of earnings from labor is on a par with forced labor."

His reasoning is simple: If a person has the right to control their own life and labor, then taxing their income without their consent is effectively compelling them to work for others. Nozick sees this as a violation of self-ownership.

The Entitlement Theory of Justice: Who Owns What?

Nozick developed what he called the entitlement theory of justice, which rejects redistributive policies in favor of strict property rights. He argues that a person is entitled to their holdings if they were:

Acquired justly (through voluntary exchange or original acquisition).

Transferred justly (through trade or gifts, not theft or coercion).

If wealth is acquired and transferred fairly, then no state has the right to interfere with how it is used. Even extreme inequalities in wealth are not unjust, so long as they arose from voluntary exchange.

In contrast to Rawls, who argued that justice requires redistribution to benefit the least advantaged, Nozick insists that any redistribution beyond voluntary charity is a violation of individual liberty.

For Nozick, the minimal state is not just a preference—it is the only morally defensible form of government. Anything beyond that, he argues, turns the government into a violator of rights rather than a protector of them.

Friedrich Hayek and the Case Against Government Planning

While Nozick provides a moral justification for minimal government, Friedrich Hayek (1899–1992) provides the economic argument. Hayek was one of the most influential economists and political theorists of the 20th century, and his critiques of central planning and government intervention helped define modern libertarian thought.

The Fatal Conceit: Why Governments Cannot Plan Economies

Hayek's most famous argument, developed in The Road to Serfdom (1944) and The Fatal Conceit (1988), is that centralized economic planning leads inevitably to oppression and economic failure.

Governments, he argues, simply do not have enough knowledge to efficiently plan economies. Unlike individual actors in a free market, bureaucrats cannot respond dynamically to changing conditions, consumer demands, and resource scarcities. The more the state tries to control economic outcomes, the more it disrupts the spontaneous order of the market.

Hayek viewed free markets as an information system—prices emerge as signals that reflect supply, demand, and relative scarcity. When governments interfere—by setting prices, controlling wages, or subsidizing industries—they distort these signals, leading to inefficiency and waste.

His greatest fear was that government intervention in the economy would eventually lead to political tyranny. In The Road to Serfdom, he warned that even well-intentioned economic policies—such as wealth redistribution and government-managed industries—could create a slippery slope toward authoritarianism.

"The more the state 'plans,' the more difficult planning becomes for the individual."

For Hayek, the free market is not just an economic tool—it is a safeguard against oppression. When people are free to buy, sell, and work as they choose, they are free in the truest political sense.

Libertarianism in Practice: The Free-Market State

Libertarian principles have profoundly shaped modern political debates, particularly in areas such as:

Taxation – Arguments for lower taxes, flat taxes, and minimal government spending.

Deregulation – Opposition to government controls on businesses and trade.

Private Property Rights – Defending property ownership as the foundation of freedom.

Abolition of Welfare States – Criticism of government welfare programs as coercive and inefficient.

Civil Liberties – Strong advocacy for free speech, gun rights, and personal autonomy.

Libertarian ideals have influenced policies in countries such as the United States, the United Kingdom, and Hong Kong, where free-market reforms have been implemented with varying degrees of success. However, critics argue that pure libertarianism fails to address issues of economic inequality, public goods, and social justice.

Conclusion: The Debate Over Minimal Government

Libertarianism remains one of the most compelling—and controversial—political philosophies of the modern era. Its defenders see it as the ultimate defense of individual freedom, while its critics argue that it neglects social obligations and collective well-being.

Nozick's argument for self-ownership and property rights challenges the very foundation of the welfare state. Hayek's critique of government planning warns against the unintended consequences of economic intervention.

But the question remains: How much government is too much? Should the state provide only the bare minimum, or does true freedom require some level of collective support? This debate continues to shape economic policy, political movements, and the fundamental question of what it means to be free.

Conservatism and Tradition

Burke, Oakeshott, and the Role of Social Stability in Governance

There are few political philosophies as misunderstood as conservatism. To some, it represents a resistance to change, a rigid defense of outdated traditions, and a refusal to embrace progress. To others, it is the bedrock of political stability, an ideology that values the accumulated wisdom of the past and warns against the reckless pursuit of utopian visions.

At its core, conservatism is not a fixed doctrine but an attitude toward change—a belief that societies should evolve organically rather than be forcibly reshaped according to abstract theories. Unlike liberalism, which prioritizes individual autonomy, or socialism, which seeks economic equality, conservatism emphasizes the importance of continuity, social cohesion, and inherited institutions. It argues that political order is fragile and that radical reforms often produce unintended consequences far worse than the problems they aim to solve.

Two of the most influential conservative thinkers, Edmund Burke (1729-1797) and Michael Oakeshott (1901-1990), articulated these ideas in ways that continue to shape political thought today. Their defenses of tradition, gradual reform, and skepticism toward abstract rationalism remain central to contemporary conservative movements.

To understand conservatism, we must explore Burke's reaction to the French Revolution, Oakeshott's philosophy of tradition and practical knowledge, and the broader conservative commitment to social stability as the foundation of governance.

Edmund Burke: The Father of Modern Conservatism

If one thinker can be credited with founding modern conservatism, it is Edmund Burke. Though he lived in the 18th century, his arguments remain strikingly relevant. His seminal work, Reflections on the Revolution in France (1790), was not just a critique of the French Revolution—it was a defense of an entire way of thinking about politics.

The Dangers of Revolutionary Change

Burke was not opposed to all change. In fact, he had supported the American Revolution and was a strong advocate for gradual reform. However, he saw in the French Revolution a dangerous experiment in radical social engineering—a movement that sought to destroy centuries of tradition overnight and replace it with abstract ideals of liberty and equality.

To Burke, this was folly of the highest order. Societies, he argued, are not mathematical equations that can be rearranged according to intellectual designs. They are organic entities, built up over generations through trial and error. Institutions—monarchy, the church, the legal system—may be imperfect, but they contain the accumulated wisdom of history. To tear them down in pursuit of theoretical perfection was to invite chaos and tyranny.

"The individual is foolish, but the species is wise."

This was Burke's central insight: no single person or revolutionary group possesses enough knowledge to redesign society from scratch. Traditions and customs develop over time because they work—not because they were rationally planned.

The Social Contract as an Inheritance

Where thinkers like Hobbes, Locke, and Rousseau described the social contract as a rational agreement among individuals, Burke saw it as something far deeper:

"Society is a partnership not only between those who are living, but between those who are living, those who are dead, and those who are to be born."

For Burke, political order is not something that each generation has the right to rewrite at will. Instead, it is an inheritance, something passed down through centuries of struggle and adaptation. Institutions such as monarchy and religion, he argued, may not be perfect, but they represent stability and continuity, providing a sense of identity and meaning that cannot be replaced by revolutionary manifestos.

Michael Oakeshott: Conservatism as a Disposition

If Burke provided the moral and historical defense of conservatism, Michael Oakeshott refined its philosophical foundation. In contrast to the ideological conservatism of political movements, Oakeshott saw conservatism as a way of thinking—a disposition rather than a rigid doctrine.

Skepticism Toward Rationalism in Politics

Oakeshott's most famous work, Rationalism in Politics (1962), argues that one of the greatest dangers in modern political life is the belief that society can be designed and perfected through abstract reason.

For Oakeshott, modern politics is dominated by rationalists—thinkers who believe that politics is like engineering, something that can be planned and executed with precision. The rationalist, Oakeshott claims, sees tradition as an obstacle to be cleared away, replacing it with rational, scientific policies that promise efficiency and progress.

But Oakeshott warns that this is a dangerous illusion. Politics is not an engineering problem; it is an ongoing conversation between generations, a process of negotiation, compromise, and adaptation.

Societies are complex, built on customs and institutions that cannot be reduced to simple formulas.

"To be conservative, then, is to prefer the familiar to the unknown, to prefer the tried to the untried, fact to mystery, the actual to the possible."

This is not a rejection of all change—rather, it is a caution against reckless reform. The conservative, in Oakeshott's view, does not oppose progress but insists that change should be gradual, incremental, and rooted in experience rather than theory.

Tradition as Practical Knowledge

One of Oakeshott's most profound insights is his distinction between technical knowledge and practical knowledge.

Technical knowledge consists of rules, formulas, and explicit instructions—it is the kind of knowledge you find in textbooks.

Practical knowledge, on the other hand, is embedded in experience—it is the kind of wisdom that cannot be written down but is learned through doing.

Oakeshott argues that societies function primarily through practical knowledge. Traditions, customs, and inherited institutions embody wisdom that no individual can fully articulate but that has stood the test of time. To discard them in favor of abstract theories is to risk losing something invaluable.

The Role of Social Stability in Governance

Both Burke and Oakeshott emphasize the need for stability in political life. Unlike progressives and revolutionaries, who see history as a march toward a better future, conservatives believe that rapid change can undermine the foundations of society, leading to disorder and unintended consequences.

Institutions as Safeguards Against Tyranny

Paradoxically, conservatism's commitment to stability often serves as a defense against tyranny. When institutions are weakened, when traditions are disregarded, power tends to accumulate in the hands of those who promise quick solutions. History has repeatedly shown that political upheaval often leads to autocratic rule—from the French Revolution's descent into the Reign of Terror to the rise of totalitarian regimes in the 20th century.

By preserving institutions—even imperfect ones—conservatives argue that society remains resilient against authoritarianism.

The Danger of Overreaching Government

Another key conservative concern is the expansion of government power in the name of progress. Whether in the form of welfare programs, economic regulations, or social engineering projects, conservatives warn that government intervention often creates more problems than it solves.

Burke worried about centralized power destroying local traditions and social cohesion.

Oakeshott warned against policymakers who believe they can reshape society like an architect designing a city.

Conservatism, in this sense, is a philosophy of limits—a recognition that human nature is flawed, knowledge is imperfect, and government power must always be restrained.

Conclusion: The Enduring Appeal of Conservatism

In a world of rapid technological and social change, conservatism remains a vital counterbalance. It reminds us that traditions matter, that institutions are fragile, and that progress should be pursued carefully rather than recklessly.

Burke and Oakeshott offer a powerful defense of gradual, organic change, rejecting both reactionary nostalgia and revolutionary zeal. Their insights continue to shape debates over governance, social policy, and the limits of state power.

Ultimately, conservatism asks a simple but profound question: What must we preserve so that we do not lose ourselves?

Theories of Democracy

Direct vs. Representative Democracy, Participatory Democracy, and Modern Democratic Thought

Democracy is among the most celebrated and debated political ideas in history. It is the rallying cry of revolutions, the ideal of constitutional governance, and the foundation of modern political legitimacy. Yet, despite its widespread acceptance, democracy is neither a singular nor a static concept. It has evolved across centuries, adapting to the demands of different societies, political institutions, and cultural contexts.

At its heart, democracy is about power and participation—who rules, how decisions are made, and what mechanisms ensure fairness and accountability. While the principle of popular sovereignty—the idea that government derives its legitimacy from the will of the people—is common to all democratic theories, how this principle is applied varies significantly. From the direct assemblies of ancient Athens to the representative governments of the modern world, from participatory experiments in local governance to digital-era democratic innovations, different models of democracy have emerged, each with distinct strengths and weaknesses.

Understanding democracy requires an examination of its historical roots, theoretical distinctions, and contemporary challenges. This chapter will explore the key forms of democracy—direct, representative, and participatory—and assess their relevance in the 21st century.

Direct Democracy: The Athenian Ideal and Its Challenges

The idea of democracy originates from ancient Greece, particularly in 5th-century BCE Athens, where it was practiced in its most direct form. The term demokratia itself comes from the Greek words demos (people) and kratos (power), meaning "rule by the people."

How Direct Democracy Worked in Athens

Athenian democracy was radically participatory. Citizens did not elect representatives to govern on their behalf; instead, they directly debated and voted on laws and policies in the Ekklesia, an assembly open to all eligible male citizens.

Key features of Athenian direct democracy included:

The Assembly (Ekklesia): The central decision-making body where citizens voted on laws, foreign policy, and other state matters.

Sortition (Random Selection): Many government positions were filled by lottery rather than election, ensuring broad civic participation.

Citizen Juries: Large juries, sometimes consisting of hundreds of citizens, decided legal cases rather than professional judges.

This system empowered ordinary citizens but also had limitations—women, slaves, and non-citizens were excluded, and the logistics of gathering large assemblies made decision-making cumbersome.

Modern Examples of Direct Democracy

While large-scale direct democracy is impractical in modern nation-states, elements of it survive in certain political systems:

Switzerland: Regular referendums allow citizens to vote on specific laws and constitutional amendments.

State and Local Referendums (U.S., U.K., etc.): Citizens in various countries vote on issues like taxation, same-sex marriage, and Brexit.

Direct democracy remains idealized for its inclusivity and transparency, but critics argue that complex modern societies require more structured governance. Many also worry about populism and the influence of misinformation, particularly in the digital age.

Representative Democracy: Balancing Participation and Practicality

As societies grew larger and more complex, direct democracy became increasingly difficult to maintain. This led to the development of representative democracy, where citizens elect officials to govern on their behalf.

This model, which emerged prominently in the 18th and 19th centuries, was influenced by Enlightenment thinkers like John Locke, Montesquieu, and James Madison, who sought a system that combined popular sovereignty with stability and institutional checks.

Key Features of Representative Democracy

Elected Legislatures – Citizens vote for representatives who propose, debate, and pass laws in bodies like parliaments or congresses.

Separation of Powers – Inspired by Montesquieu, modern democracies divide power among executive, legislative, and judicial branches to prevent tyranny.

Periodic Elections – Leaders are held accountable through regular, competitive elections.

Rule of Law and Rights Protection – Constitutions and legal frameworks protect minorities and prevent majoritarian abuses.

Strengths and Weaknesses of Representative Democracy

Advantages

Scalability: Works for large populations and diverse societies.

Expertise: Elected officials often have more knowledge of governance than the average citizen.

Stability: Institutions prevent hasty decisions driven by emotional public reactions.

Criticisms

Elitism and Political Alienation: Elected officials may serve their own interests or those of elites rather than the people.

Voter Apathy: Citizens feel disconnected from decision-making, reducing engagement.

Corruption and Special Interests: Lobbyists and corporations influence politicians, distorting democratic ideals.

Modern representative democracies—such as those in the United States, United Kingdom, Germany, and India—struggle with these challenges, leading some to advocate for greater citizen participation beyond periodic elections.

Participatory Democracy: Beyond Elections

In response to the limitations of both direct and representative democracy, some political theorists and activists have championed participatory democracy—a system that encourages continuous citizen involvement in decision-making.

This idea gained prominence during the civil rights movements of the 1960s, particularly in the work of scholars like Carole Pateman. Unlike representative democracy, where participation is mostly passive (limited to voting every few years), participatory democracy seeks to empower citizens through active engagement in governance.

Key Features of Participatory Democracy

Local governance involvement: Neighborhood councils, town hall meetings, and citizen assemblies give people direct input on policies.

Deliberative democracy: Citizens discuss and debate policies in structured forums before decisions are made.

Participatory budgeting: Communities decide how public funds are allocated (e.g., in Brazil's Porto Alegre).

Citizen juries and panels: Groups of randomly selected citizens review laws and advise policymakers.

Can Participatory Democracy Work on a Large Scale?

While participatory democracy strengthens civic engagement,

skeptics argue that it works best at local levels but struggles at national scales. Large populations make widespread deliberation logistically difficult, and many citizens lack the time or interest to engage deeply in governance.

However, new technologies—digital democracy platforms, online petitions, and crowd-sourced policymaking—are opening new possibilities for scaling participatory democracy in the 21st century.

Modern Democratic Thought: Challenges and Future Directions

Challenges Facing Democracy Today

Even in well-established democracies, democratic backsliding and disillusionment have become pressing concerns. Several challenges threaten the legitimacy and functionality of democratic systems:

Populism – Leaders who bypass democratic institutions and appeal directly to "the people" can weaken checks and balances.

Misinformation and Media Manipulation – Social media and biased news sources shape public opinion, sometimes at the expense of rational debate and informed decision-making.

Economic Inequality – Disparities in wealth translate to disparities in political influence, undermining democratic fairness.

Voter Suppression and Electoral Manipulation – Gerrymandering, restrictive voting laws, and flawed electoral systems weaken democratic participation.

The Future of Democracy

As democracy faces these crises, new theories and innovations are emerging:

Digital Democracy: Online tools enabling greater political engagement and direct participation.

Deliberative Democracy: Enhancing the quality of public debate by fostering informed, structured discussions.

Hybrid Models: Combining elements of direct, representative, and participatory democracy to create more responsive systems.

Conclusion: Democracy as an Evolving Ideal

Democracy is not a fixed system but an ongoing experiment. From the Athenian assemblies to modern digital platforms, its forms have changed, yet its fundamental principles—popular sovereignty, accountability, and political participation—remain central to the governance of free societies.

The challenge for the future is not merely to preserve democracy but to revitalize it, ensuring that it remains resilient, inclusive, and truly representative in an era of global complexity and rapid technological change.

Critiques of Democracy

Plato's Critique, Schumpeter's Elitist Theory, and Contemporary Concerns

Democracy is often regarded as the pinnacle of political progress—a system that guarantees freedom, ensures accountability, and reflects the will of the people. It is championed as the fairest form of government, one that upholds equality, participation, and human rights. And yet, throughout history, democracy has faced profound criticism, not just from dictators or authoritarians but from some of the greatest minds in political philosophy.

From Plato's philosophical rejection of mass rule to Joseph Schumpeter's realist defense of elitism, critics of democracy have raised difficult questions:

Can ordinary citizens govern themselves wisely?

Do democratic elections actually reflect the best interests of the people?

Does democracy inevitably lead to mediocrity, instability, or even tyranny?

In modern times, concerns about populism, polarization, corporate influence, and voter manipulation have fueled debates about whether democracy is in decline or if it was always flawed to begin with. While democracy remains the dominant form of government in much of the world, its vulnerabilities deserve serious examination.

This chapter explores three major critiques: Plato's warning about democracy's inherent instability, Schumpeter's argument for elitist rule, and contemporary concerns about democracy's functionality in the modern world.

Plato's Critique: Democracy as a Path to Tyranny

Few thinkers have been as critical of democracy as Plato (427–347 BCE). Writing during a time of political instability in ancient Athens, Plato witnessed firsthand how democracy could lead to disaster. His mentor, Socrates, was sentenced to death by a democratic vote—an event that deeply shaped Plato's skepticism of popular rule.

Plato's critique of democracy appears most forcefully in The Republic, where he argues that democracy is inherently flawed because it places power in the hands of the ignorant masses rather than the wise and virtuous few.

The Flaws of Democracy According to Plato

Plato's fundamental criticism is that democracy leads to rule by the uninformed. He compares democracy to a ship without a skilled captain, where the crew (the masses) overthrows the navigator (the expert) and makes decisions based on popularity rather than wisdom.

His key concerns include:

The Rule of the Unqualified – Plato believed that politics requires expertise, just as medicine requires trained doctors or architecture requires skilled builders. In a democracy, however, leaders are chosen based on popularity rather than competence, leading to poor governance.

Excessive Freedom and Chaos – Democracies emphasize personal freedom, but Plato saw this as a double-edged sword. Too much liberty, he argued, leads to lawlessness, selfishness, and a breakdown of social order.

Demagoguery and Populism – In a democracy, skilled orators and manipulative politicians can deceive the masses, making false promises and appealing to emotions rather than reason. This paves the way for corrupt and dangerous leaders.

Democracy as the Road to Tyranny – According to Plato, democracy is not stable. Over time, the people, craving order after experiencing chaos, may willingly hand power to a dictator. This leads to the rise of a tyrant, making democracy self-destructive.

Plato famously classified democracy as one of the lowest forms of government, just one step away from tyranny. He proposed an alternative model: rule by philosopher-kings, wise rulers trained in logic, ethics, and political philosophy who would govern not for their own benefit but for the good of the people.

Though Plato's vision of philosopher-kings is highly utopian and unrealistic, his concerns about demagoguery, incompetence, and the fragility of democratic rule remain strikingly relevant today.

Schumpeter's Elitist Theory: Democracy as a Competition for Leadership

If Plato saw democracy as chaotic and self-destructive, Joseph Schumpeter (1883–1950) viewed it as a necessary but deeply flawed system that should be approached with realism, not idealism.

Schumpeter, an Austrian political economist, challenged the classical idea that democracy reflects the "will of the people." Instead, he argued that democracy is really a competition between elites for power, with the public playing a largely passive role.

Democracy as an Elitist System

In his seminal work, Capitalism, Socialism, and Democracy (1942), Schumpeter rejects the idea that voters are rational actors who make informed choices based on reasoned debate. Instead, he describes democracy as a process where:

Political elites (leaders, parties, and interest groups) compete for power through elections.

Citizens do not truly shape policy; they simply choose between competing elites, much like consumers choosing between brands.

The masses are too uninformed, irrational, and easily manipulated to engage in serious political decision-making.

For Schumpeter, democracy is best understood not as "rule by the people" but as a method for selecting rulers. His elitist theory suggests that democratic governance is most stable when competent elites manage the state, while the public's role is largely passive.

This view challenges romanticized ideas of democracy and aligns with modern concerns about media influence, voter ignorance, and corporate control of politics.

Schumpeter's Warnings and Contemporary Relevance

Schumpeter's elitist view of democracy is controversial, but his concerns are echoed in modern political realities:

Low voter engagement: In many democracies, voter turnout is shockingly low, reflecting apathy or a belief that votes do not truly change policy.

Manipulation by media and corporations: Political campaigns are shaped by advertising, marketing, and propaganda, making elections more about persuasion than genuine debate.

Power of unelected elites: Even in democracies, bureaucrats, corporate executives, and international institutions wield massive influence that is not subject to democratic control.

Schumpeter forces us to ask: Is democracy really about "the

people," or is it simply a game played by elites?

Contemporary Concerns: Is Democracy Failing?

Beyond Plato and Schumpeter, modern political theorists, journalists, and activists have raised urgent concerns about whether democracy is still functional in the 21st century.

Key Challenges Facing Democracy Today

Rise of Populism – Leaders like Donald Trump, Jair Bolsonaro, and Viktor Orbán have used democratic elections to gain power but then weaken democratic institutions once in office.

Misinformation and Social Media – The rise of fake news, echo chambers, and algorithm-driven content has made informed democratic debate harder than ever.

Economic Inequality and Corporate Influence – The wealthiest individuals and corporations exert disproportionate influence over policy through lobbying, campaign financing, and media control.

Voter Apathy and Disillusionment – Many citizens feel disconnected from politics, believing that voting changes little. This fuels low turnout and disengagement.

Can Democracy Be Reformed?

Some propose reforms to strengthen democracy, including:

Deliberative democracy – Structured citizen assemblies to improve public decision-making.

Campaign finance reform – Reducing the influence of money in politics.

Stronger civic education – Teaching critical thinking to combat misinformation.

But the bigger question remains: Can democracy survive its own flaws, or are we heading toward a post-democratic world?

Conclusion: Democracy's Future in a World of Uncertainty

Plato saw democracy as a stepping stone to tyranny. Schumpeter viewed it as rule by elites, disguised as popular sovereignty. Today, we see democracy struggling under the weight of populism, misinformation, and economic inequality.

And yet, despite its flaws, democracy endures. It remains the most widely accepted form of government, even as its weaknesses become more apparent. The challenge for the future is not merely to defend democracy, but to rethink and reform it so that it remains resilient in the face of modern threats.

Does democracy have a future? Or are its critics correct in saying that it is an unstable experiment, destined to fail? The answer is still unfolding.

Totalitarianism and Authoritarianism

Fascism, Stalinism, and the Mechanisms of Oppressive Rule

If democracy represents the hope for a government of the people, by the people, and for the people, then totalitarianism and authoritarianism represent its antithesis—the rule of the few, enforced through oppression, violence, and absolute control. These systems emerge in times of political upheaval, economic instability, and social disintegration, offering the illusion of order at the cost of freedom.

Totalitarian and authoritarian regimes share certain fundamental traits: centralized power, suppression of dissent, and a disregard for democratic institutions. But they are not identical. Totalitarianism seeks total domination of public and private life, whereas authoritarianism tolerates limited individual freedoms as long as the state remains unchallenged.

This chapter explores the differences between totalitarianism and authoritarianism, examines two of history's most infamous totalitarian ideologies—Fascism and Stalinism—and analyzes the mechanisms by which oppressive rule is maintained.

Totalitarianism vs. Authoritarianism: Understanding Oppression

Both totalitarianism and authoritarianism are forms of non-democratic rule, but they differ in their ambitions, methods, and ideological commitments.

Authoritarianism: Control Without Ideological Absolutism

An authoritarian regime is characterized by:

Strong central power – The state is controlled by a leader or small ruling elite.

Limited political freedoms – Opposition parties, free press, and civil liberties are restricted but not entirely abolished.

No total control over society – Citizens may retain private freedoms (economic, religious, cultural) as long as they do not threaten the state.

Use of repression – Censorship, political imprisonment, and coercion are common tools to suppress dissent.

Examples of authoritarian regimes include:

Francisco Franco's Spain (1939–1975) – A dictatorship with conservative-nationalist rule but without a radical vision for society.

Augusto Pinochet's Chile (1973–1990) – A military regime that curtailed political freedoms while allowing economic liberalization.

Modern-day Russia under Vladimir Putin – A government that suppresses opposition while maintaining elements of electoral democracy.

Totalitarianism: Absolute Domination of Life

A totalitarian regime, by contrast, seeks complete control over society, including the thoughts, behaviors, and beliefs of its people. It is characterized by:

An all-encompassing ideology – The regime justifies its existence through a grand ideological vision (e.g., racial supremacy, class struggle).

Total political control – One-party rule eliminates opposition, controls elections, and dictates policy.

State control over society – The government dominates not just politics, but economy, culture, education, and even private life.

Mass surveillance and terror – Citizens are constantly monitored, dissent is met with brutal punishment, and loyalty to the regime is enforced through fear.

The two most infamous totalitarian regimes of the 20th century—Fascist Italy/Nazi Germany and Stalinist Soviet Union—demonstrated how such systems can rise, consolidate power, and maintain control through propaganda, violence, and mass mobilization.

Fascism: The Politics of Ultra-Nationalism and Militarism

Fascism is one of the most aggressive and destructive totalitarian ideologies in history. Rooted in extreme nationalism, militarism, and an obsession with strength and order, fascist regimes seek to unify the nation under an authoritarian leader while violently eliminating opposition.

The Rise of Fascism: Mussolini and Hitler

Fascism emerged in the early 20th century as a response to political instability, economic crises, and fears of communism. It promised to restore national strength through absolute control, mobilization of the masses, and warlike expansionism.

Benito Mussolini (Italy, 1922–1943) – The first self-proclaimed fascist leader, Mussolini centralized power, abolished opposition, and introduced the corporate state, in which the economy was controlled by the state but remained privately owned.

Adolf Hitler (Germany, 1933–1945) – Hitler's Nazi regime expanded Mussolini's model, incorporating racial supremacy, anti-Semitism, and a war-driven economy. The result was World War II and the Holocaust, where six million Jews and millions of others were exterminated.

Core Characteristics of Fascist Rule

Fascist governments maintain power through:

Cult of the Leader – Leaders like Mussolini and Hitler presented themselves as infallible, god-like figures, demanding personal loyalty above all else.

State-Controlled Propaganda – Fascist regimes used radio, newspapers, and mass rallies to spread nationalist ideology and demonize enemies.

Militarization of Society – Fascist states glorified war, imposed strict discipline, and indoctrinated youth through paramilitary organizations.

Suppression of Dissent – Opponents were imprisoned, exiled, or executed. Secret police (e.g., the Gestapo in Nazi Germany) ensured absolute obedience.

Economic and Social Control – While fascists allowed private enterprise, all major industries were directed toward nationalist and military goals.

Though Nazi Germany was destroyed in 1945, fascist and neo-fascist movements continue to emerge, often disguised under nationalist populism and anti-immigrant sentiment.

Stalinism: The Communist Nightmare

Where fascism is rooted in ultra-nationalism, Stalinism—named after Soviet dictator Joseph Stalin (1878–1953)—was a radical left-wing totalitarian system justified by class struggle and socialist revolution.

How Stalin Transformed Communism into a Totalitarian State

The original vision of communism, as proposed by Karl Marx, envisioned a classless, stateless society based on collective ownership. But under Stalin's rule in the USSR (1924–1953), communism became a totalitarian nightmare, marked by:

The Cult of Personality – Stalin was glorified as a near-divine leader, depicted as the sole savior of the Soviet Union.

The Purges and Show Trials – Stalin's political paranoia led to the Great Purge (1936–1938), during which millions of supposed "enemies of the state" were executed or sent to forced labor camps (Gulags).

State-Controlled Economy – Through Five-Year Plans, Stalin industrialized the Soviet economy but at a devastating human cost, including mass famine in Ukraine (Holodomor, 1932–1933).

Total Suppression of Dissent – The secret police (NKVD) arrested, tortured, and executed intellectuals, military leaders, and political rivals.

Control Over Thought and Culture – Art, literature, and education were strictly censored to align with state propaganda.

Stalin's totalitarian model was replicated in Maoist China, North Korea, and Eastern Bloc countries, showing how socialist ideology could be distorted into authoritarian control.

The Mechanisms of Oppressive Rule

Despite differences in ideology, all totalitarian and authoritarian regimes use common tactics to maintain power:

Surveillance and Informants – Secret police and mass surveillance ensure that dissenters are identified and punished.

State-Controlled Media – Censorship and propaganda shape public perception, eliminating opposition narratives.

Indoctrination and Education Control – Schools, universities, and youth organizations enforce loyalty to the regime.

Force and Fear – Political prisons, forced labor camps, and executions intimidate citizens into submission.

These tactics ensure that once authoritarianism takes hold, it is incredibly difficult to dislodge.

Conclusion: The Ever-Present Threat of Oppressive Rule

Totalitarianism and authoritarianism did not end with Hitler and Stalin. Modern regimes in North Korea, China, and Russia continue to use many of the same mechanisms of control, even as they adopt new technological tools such as digital surveillance and AI-driven propaganda.

The challenge for modern political philosophy is to understand how oppressive rule emerges and how it can be prevented. If democracy is to survive, it must recognize the dangers of unchecked power, mass manipulation, and the allure of absolute authority—because, as history shows, freedom is always vulnerable to those who seek to control it.

Populism and the Crisis of Democracy

Left-Wing vs. Right-Wing Populism, Demagoguery, and the Role of Media

The story of democracy is, at its core, a story of trust—trust in institutions, in elected representatives, and in the mechanisms that turn the collective will into effective governance. Yet in modern times, that trust has been eroding, chipped away by economic discontent, political polarization, and a growing sense that the people in power no longer represent the interests of ordinary citizens. In this void of trust, populism thrives.

Populism is not a political ideology in itself. It is, rather, a mode of political engagement—a rhetorical style and a strategic approach to power that divides the world into two opposing camps: "the pure people" versus "the corrupt elite." It is fueled by disillusionment with traditional political parties and institutions, offering simple, emotionally charged solutions to complex problems. And while it can emerge on both the left and the right, its manifestations, goals, and dangers vary widely.

The rise of populist movements across the world—from Donald Trump in the United States and Jair Bolsonaro in Brazil to Podemos in Spain and Hugo Chávez in Venezuela—has raised urgent questions about the health of democracy itself. Does populism revitalize democracy by bringing the concerns of the people to the forefront? Or does it, by its very nature, corrode democratic norms, replacing reasoned debate with raw emotion, constitutional governance with personalist rule?

To answer these questions, we must examine the nature of populism, its left-wing and right-wing variants, the role of demagoguery, and the ways in which modern media—especially social media—have accelerated its spread.

The Nature of Populism: The People vs. The Elite

At its heart, populism is defined by a binary worldview:

The "people" are presented as a morally pure and unified group, often depicted as hardworking, virtuous, and exploited.

The "elite" is portrayed as corrupt, self-serving, and detached from the struggles of ordinary citizens.

This framing is what makes populism so potent. It taps into real grievances, whether economic, cultural, or political, and channels them into a narrative that explains who is to blame and who can fix it.

Populists claim that they alone speak for "the real people." This leads to a dangerous logic: if they are the true voice of the people, then any opposition must, by definition, be working against the people's interests. This mindset is inherently anti-pluralistic—it rejects compromise, dismisses dissent, and often undermines democratic checks and balances.

Yet, populism is not inherently left-wing or right-wing. Its character is shaped by what grievances it responds to and who it defines as "the enemy."

Left-Wing vs. Right-Wing Populism

Though they share a rhetorical structure, left-wing and right-wing populisms emerge from different political traditions and social anxieties.

Left-Wing Populism: The People vs. the Economic Elite

Left-wing populism is primarily concerned with economic inequality, class struggle, and corporate power. It sees the "elite" as an economic oligarchy—wealthy corporations, financial institutions, and the political establishment that serves them.

Notable left-wing populist leaders include:

Hugo Chávez (Venezuela) – Used populist rhetoric to mobilize working-class resentment against wealthy elites and foreign corporations, leading to state-controlled industries and social welfare programs.

Bernie Sanders (United States) – Framed his campaigns around opposition to billionaires and corporate influence in politics, advocating for universal healthcare and wealth redistribution.

Podemos (Spain) – A left-populist party that emerged in response to economic crises, calling for democratic renewal and financial regulation.

Left-wing populists often appeal to workers, students, and marginalized groups, arguing that the economic system is rigged against them and that radical redistribution of wealth is necessary for justice.

However, when left-wing populism turns authoritarian—as seen in Venezuela under Nicolás Maduro—it can result in economic mismanagement, state repression, and the erosion of democratic institutions under the guise of protecting the people.

Right-Wing Populism: The People vs. Cultural and Political Enemies

Right-wing populism, by contrast, is often driven by cultural and nationalistic concerns rather than economic grievances. It portrays the elite as out-of-touch politicians, globalists, intellectuals, and immigrants who are undermining national identity, traditional values, and sovereignty.

Notable right-wing populist figures include:

Donald Trump (United States) – Framed his movement as a defense of "real Americans" against corrupt Washington elites, the mainstream media, and immigrants.

Jair Bolsonaro (Brazil) – Capitalized on fears of crime, corruption, and leftist politics, promising to restore order through nationalism and strongman leadership.

Marine Le Pen (France) – Leads a nationalist movement focused on restricting immigration and resisting European Union influence.

Right-wing populists often appeal to rural communities, traditionalists, and nationalist movements, arguing that their way of life is under attack from cultural outsiders, progressive elites, or international organizations.

When right-wing populism escalates, it can lead to xenophobia, suppression of dissent, and democratic backsliding, as seen in Hungary under Viktor Orbán, where independent media and judicial institutions have been systematically undermined.

The Role of Demagoguery: How Populists Gain Power

A populist leader is often, by necessity, a demagogue—someone who stirs up public emotion to gain power rather than engaging in rational debate. The best demagogues have an intuitive sense of what their followers fear and desire, and they craft simple, compelling narratives to harness that energy.

Common demagogic tactics include:

Scapegoating – Blaming social problems on a specific group (e.g., immigrants, corporations, globalists, the media).

Anti-Intellectualism – Dismissing experts and institutions as part of the corrupt elite.

Emotional Appeals – Relying on fear, nostalgia, or anger rather than facts or policy discussions.

Attacking the Press – Labeling unfavorable media as "fake news" or "the enemy of the people."

Undermining Elections – Suggesting that elections are rigged if the populist does not win.

The danger of demagoguery is that it erodes trust in democratic processes, making the public more receptive to authoritarian solutions.

The Role of Media in Populism's Rise

No phenomenon has accelerated the spread of populism more

than modern media, especially social media. In the past, populists relied on mass rallies, radio, and newspapers to spread their message. Today, Twitter, Facebook, and YouTube provide instant, unfiltered access to millions.

Key ways media fuels populism:

Algorithmic Polarization – Social media feeds reinforce users' existing beliefs, pushing them deeper into ideological bubbles.

Disinformation – False or misleading content spreads rapidly, shaping public perception.

Direct Leader-to-Public Communication – Populists bypass traditional media, speaking directly to their followers.

Outrage and Virality – Controversial statements, even if false, dominate the news cycle and increase political engagement.

Donald Trump's presidency illustrated the power of social media populism, where tweets became policy announcements, and fact-checking was dismissed as establishment bias.

Conclusion: Populism's Challenge to Democracy

Populism presents a paradox. On the one hand, it exposes real failures of democratic governance, forcing mainstream politicians to address public grievances. On the other, it can undermine democracy itself by fostering division, weakening institutions, and concentrating power in charismatic leaders.

Whether populism strengthens or destroys democracy depends on how societies respond. Do they address the legitimate concerns that fuel populism, or do they allow demagogues to exploit anger for personal gain?

The challenge of the 21st century is not just to defend democracy, but to rebuild trust in it—before populism consumes it entirely.

The Role of Law in Politics

Natural Law vs. Legal Positivism, the Rule of Law, and Constitutionalism

Politics and law are deeply intertwined. While politics determines who holds power and how they exercise it, law defines the boundaries within which that power operates. A society without laws is mere anarchy, but a society where law is subservient to raw power is mere despotism. Law, in its ideal form, is meant to structure governance, protect rights, and uphold justice. Yet, the nature of law—what it is, where it comes from, and how it should function—has been a topic of philosophical debate for centuries.

Does law derive from an objective moral order, as natural law theorists argue? Or is it simply a set of rules created and enforced by human institutions, as legal positivists claim? Should the law serve as an impartial guardian of justice, or is it merely an instrument of political power? How do we ensure that law restrains rulers rather than enabling them?

To explore these questions, we must delve into two fundamental theories of law—natural law and legal positivism—before examining the rule of law and the principles of constitutionalism, which serve as the cornerstones of stable, just governance.

Natural Law: Morality as the Foundation of Law

The concept of natural law suggests that law is not simply a human invention but rather a reflection of a higher moral order. Whether derived from divine will, human reason, or the very structure of nature itself, natural law theorists argue that true laws must be grounded in moral principles that exist independently of human institutions.

The Classical Origins of Natural Law

The roots of natural law theory stretch back to Ancient Greece and Rome. Plato and Aristotle argued that law must reflect justice, which is not merely a social construct but an objective reality. For Aristotle, the purpose of law was to promote human flourishing (eudaimonia) by ensuring a just and ordered society.

The most famous articulation of natural law, however, came from Cicero, the Roman statesman and philosopher, who wrote:

"True law is right reason in agreement with nature; it is of universal application, unchanging and everlasting."

Here, Cicero asserts that real laws are not simply the decrees of rulers but are discoverable through reason and must align with a universal moral order.

Aquinas and the Christian Synthesis

The medieval Christian tradition, especially in the writings of Thomas Aquinas, fused natural law theory with theological doctrine. According to Aquinas, there are different types of law:

Eternal Law – The overarching divine order governing the universe.

Natural Law – The portion of eternal law that human beings can discern through reason.

Human Law – Laws created by governments, which must align with natural law to be just.

For Aquinas, a law that contradicts moral truth is no law at all—a principle later echoed by figures such as Martin Luther King Jr., who famously stated:

"An unjust law is no law at all."

This perspective has been the foundation of human rights movements, arguing that certain rights are inherent and cannot be violated, even by legitimate governments.

Modern Natural Law Thinkers

Even in secular thought, natural law remains influential. Thinkers such as John Locke argued that human beings have natural rights to life, liberty, and property, which governments must respect. The American Declaration of Independence and the Universal Declaration of Human Rights reflect this belief in inherent, pre-political rights.

But natural law theory has faced challenges, particularly from legal positivists, who reject the idea that law is necessarily connected to morality.

Legal Positivism: Law as Human Construction

Legal positivists argue that law is what is written and enforced, regardless of its moral content. Unlike natural law theorists, they do not claim that legal systems must reflect some higher moral order—only that they must be established by recognized authorities and follow formal procedures.

Thomas Hobbes and the Sovereign's Law

One of the earliest proponents of a positivist approach was Thomas Hobbes, who argued in Leviathan that law is simply the command of the sovereign. For Hobbes, legal order is essential because, without it, humanity would be trapped in a brutal state of nature—a war of all against all. Whether laws are just or unjust is irrelevant; what matters is that they maintain order and prevent chaos.

John Austin: The Command Theory of Law

Legal positivism was later systematized by John Austin, who defined law as:

"A command issued by the sovereign, backed by the threat of sanction."

For Austin, the law is not about morality but about obedience and enforcement. A law's legitimacy does not come from its justice but from the fact that it is recognized and imposed by the ruling authority.

H.L.A. Hart: The Rules of Law

In the 20th century, H.L.A. Hart refined legal positivism by arguing that law is not just about commands but about a system of primary and secondary rules:

Primary rules regulate behavior (e.g., criminal laws, traffic laws).

Secondary rules establish how laws are created, interpreted, and enforced (e.g., constitutional rules, judicial review).

Hart's legal positivism acknowledges that legal systems require stability and internal logic, but it does not require them to be morally just. This idea explains why laws can be oppressive yet still be "valid" in a technical sense.

The Rule of Law: Restraining Power

If legal positivism is correct that laws exist independently of morality, then what stops governments from creating unjust or oppressive laws? The answer lies in the rule of law—the idea that all laws must be applied fairly, consistently, and impartially, even to those in power.

The rule of law, as articulated by thinkers like John Locke and A.V. Dicey, includes key principles:

No one is above the law – Even government officials must follow the law.

Laws must be publicly known and predictable – Secret laws or arbitrary enforcement undermine justice.

Legal processes must be fair and impartial – Courts must be independent, and trials must be just.

Where the rule of law breaks down, tyranny emerges. When laws are mere tools of rulers rather than safeguards for society, democracy collapses into authoritarianism.

Constitutionalism: The Structure of Political Law

If the rule of law is about fair enforcement, constitutionalism is about defining the limits of power. A constitution provides:

A framework for governance (e.g., separation of powers, federalism).

Guaranteed rights and protections (e.g., freedom of speech, due process).

Mechanisms for change (e.g., amendments, judicial review).

Rigid vs. Flexible Constitutions

Rigid Constitutions (e.g., U.S. Constitution) require formal amendments to change fundamental laws.

Flexible Constitutions (e.g., U.K.'s uncodified system) evolve through parliamentary decisions and legal precedents.

Both systems have strengths and weaknesses—rigid constitutions protect rights but can be difficult to adapt; flexible constitutions allow adaptation but risk instability.

Conclusion: The Role of Law in Just Governance

The debate between natural law and legal positivism continues to shape modern legal thought. While natural law argues that justice must anchor law, legal positivism insists that law is a human construct that must be obeyed regardless of morality. The rule of law and constitutionalism attempt to balance these perspectives, ensuring that law is both stable and just.

But the key challenge remains: How do we prevent law from becoming a tool of oppression rather than a guardian of freedom? The answer lies in vigilance—ensuring that laws remain just, that governments remain accountable, and that power remains constrained. For when law fails, tyranny is never far behind.

Political Economy and the State

Capitalism, Socialism, Mixed Economies, and the Role of Government in Markets

The relationship between politics and economics is one of the most consequential in human history. Every government, from ancient empires to modern nation-states, has had to determine how resources are distributed, how markets function, and how wealth is generated. The field of political economy explores these questions, examining the ways in which political structures influence economic systems—and vice versa.

At the heart of this debate are three primary economic models: capitalism, socialism, and mixed economies. Each represents a different vision of the role of government in markets, the distribution of wealth, and the nature of economic justice. While capitalism emphasizes individual enterprise and private ownership, socialism envisions a world where resources are shared more equitably, often under state control. Most nations today exist somewhere between these extremes, employing mixed economies that balance market freedom with government intervention.

Yet, beneath these economic models lies a deeper philosophical question: What is the proper role of the state in economic life? Should governments interfere in markets to protect the vulnerable, or should they let competition run its course? Should wealth be redistributed to ensure fairness, or should individuals reap the full rewards of their labor? And in an era of globalization and digital economies, do the old models still hold?

Understanding political economy is crucial because it shapes everything from social mobility and job creation to financial crises and inequality. The policies a government adopts—whether taxation, regulation, welfare, or trade agreements—directly impact the well-being of its citizens.

This chapter explores the fundamental economic models, their advantages and criticisms, and the ever-evolving role of the state in regulating and guiding economic life.

Capitalism: The Power of Markets
The Core of Capitalism

At its foundation, capitalism is an economic system based on private ownership of the means of production, free markets, and competition. It operates on the principle that when individuals and businesses are allowed to pursue their own economic self-interest, society as a whole prospers. This philosophy was famously articulated by Adam Smith in The Wealth of Nations (1776), where he described the "invisible hand" of the market—a mechanism through which individual pursuit of profit leads to collective economic benefits.

The core tenets of capitalism include:

Private Property – Individuals and businesses own land, factories, and resources rather than the state.

Free Markets – Prices and production are determined by supply and demand, not government directives.

Profit Motive – Economic activity is driven by the incentive to make a profit.

Minimal Government Intervention – The state's role is largely confined to enforcing contracts, protecting property rights, and maintaining order.

The Advantages of Capitalism

Capitalism is often credited with unparalleled economic growth and innovation. By allowing businesses to compete, it incentivizes efficiency, technological advancement, and entrepreneurship. The Industrial Revolution, the rise of Silicon Valley, and the global expansion of trade are all products of capitalist systems.

Other advantages include:

Higher Productivity – Competition forces companies to innovate and improve efficiency.

Economic Freedom – Individuals have the freedom to pursue careers, start businesses, and accumulate wealth.

Consumer Choice – Markets respond to consumer demand, leading to a diverse range of goods and services.

Criticisms of Capitalism

Despite its strengths, capitalism is not without its flaws. Critics argue that:

Inequality and Wealth Concentration – Capitalist markets tend to favor the wealthy, leading to vast disparities in income and opportunity.

Boom-and-Bust Cycles – Capitalism is prone to financial crises, as seen in the Great Depression (1929) and the Global Financial Crisis (2008).

Exploitation of Labor – Businesses seeking profit may drive down wages and working conditions.

Environmental Damage – The pursuit of growth often leads to unsustainable exploitation of natural resources.

These concerns have led many thinkers—most notably Karl Marx—to argue that capitalism, while productive, is fundamentally unjust.

Socialism: Economic Justice and Collective Ownership

The Core of Socialism

Socialism is an economic system in which the means of production—factories, land, and resources—are collectively owned or controlled by the state in order to achieve economic equality. Socialists argue that capitalism creates injustice, exploitation, and social division, and that only by redistributing wealth and resources can true fairness be achieved.

Key socialist principles include:

Public Ownership – Industries such as healthcare, education, and energy are often state-controlled.

Economic Planning – Production and distribution are determined by government planning rather than market forces.

Redistribution of Wealth – Progressive taxation and welfare systems aim to reduce economic inequality.

The Advantages of Socialism

Socialist economies prioritize social welfare, economic security, and fairness. Advocates argue that:

Basic Needs Are Met – Universal healthcare, education, and housing ensure that no one is left behind.

Greater Economic Equality – Policies like progressive taxation and social programs reduce income disparity.

Protection from Market Failures – Government intervention prevents crises caused by unregulated capitalism.

Criticisms of Socialism

Inefficiency – State-run industries often lack competition, leading to waste and stagnation.

Bureaucracy and Corruption – Large governments can become bloated and ineffective.

Lack of Innovation – Without profit incentives, there is less motivation to innovate or improve productivity.

Risk of Authoritarianism – In some cases, socialist policies have led to totalitarian state control, as seen in the Soviet Union and Maoist China.

These concerns have led many nations to adopt mixed economies rather than full socialism.

Mixed Economies: Balancing Market Freedom and Government Intervention

Most modern economies—including the United States, Germany, and Sweden—are neither purely capitalist nor socialist but a blend of both.

How Mixed Economies Work

A mixed economy preserves the benefits of capitalism—such as competition and private enterprise—while allowing for government intervention to correct market failures and provide public goods.

Common features of mixed economies include:

Private Industry with Public Regulation – Businesses operate freely, but governments regulate areas like banking, healthcare, and labor rights.

Welfare Systems – Programs like Social Security, unemployment benefits, and universal healthcare support citizens.

Public-Private Partnerships – Governments may fund infrastructure projects, subsidize education, or support research and development.

Challenges of Mixed Economies

Balancing Growth and Equality – Too much regulation can stifle economic growth, while too little can increase inequality.

Political Disputes – Governments frequently debate how much intervention is too much.

Debt and Deficits – Social programs require funding, which can lead to national debt crises if mismanaged.

Conclusion: The Role of the State in Markets

Political economy is ultimately about balance. While capitalism fosters innovation, it also creates inequality. While socialism ensures economic security, it can stifle growth and individual freedom. Most governments today seek a middle path, allowing markets to function while stepping in to correct failures.

But the debate is far from over. In an age of automation, climate change, and global financial crises, new economic models may emerge. The question is not whether government should intervene in the economy—but how much, in what ways, and to what end?

Understanding these debates is essential, for economic policies do not exist in isolation—they shape the very fabric of society itself.

Nationalism and Identity Politics

Nation-States, Ethnic Nationalism, and the Politics of Identity

Few forces have shaped modern history as profoundly as nationalism. It has inspired revolutions, fueled wars, built nations, and divided societies. It is a double-edged sword—capable of uniting people under a shared identity, yet equally capable of fostering division and conflict. Closely tied to nationalism is identity politics, which, in contemporary times, has become one of the most polarizing issues in political discourse. Whether in debates over ethnic identity, cultural heritage, or the role of race, gender, and religion in politics, identity has emerged as a powerful force shaping political movements and governance.

But what exactly is nationalism? How does it differ from identity politics? And what happens when these two forces interact? The answers to these questions lie at the heart of some of the most urgent political issues of the 21st century, from Brexit and the rise of populist nationalism to ethnic conflicts and struggles over minority rights.

To understand nationalism and identity politics, we must explore their historical roots, their philosophical justifications, and the ways in which they shape political life today.

What Is Nationalism? The Nation as a Political and Cultural Idea

At its core, nationalism is the belief that a group of people who share a common culture, language, history, or ethnicity should be united under a sovereign state. The nation is seen as the primary political unit, and nationalists argue that the political boundaries of the state should align with the cultural or ethnic boundaries of the nation.

This idea is relatively modern. In the Middle Ages, people identified more with their local communities, religious affiliations, or ruling dynasties rather than with a "nation." The rise of nationalism as a political force only took shape in the late 18th and 19th centuries, particularly with the French and American Revolutions, which emphasized self-determination and national identity as fundamental political rights.

Two Types of Nationalism: Civic vs. Ethnic

While nationalism as a whole prioritizes the nation as the central political unit, it can take radically different forms:

Civic Nationalism – Based on shared political values, institutions, and citizenship rather than ethnicity or ancestry. In this form, being part of a nation is a matter of political allegiance rather than race or culture.

Example: The United States, Canada, and France—where people of diverse ethnic backgrounds are united under a common civic identity.

Often associated with liberal democracy and the idea of a multicultural state.

Ethnic Nationalism – Defines the nation in terms of ancestry, culture, language, or religion, often leading to exclusionary politics.

Example: Germany's 19th-century nationalism, which emphasized "blood and soil" (Blut und Boden), or Japan's historical ethnic homogeneity.

Can lead to xenophobia, ethnic conflict, and even ethnic cleansing if taken to extremes.

While civic nationalism can be inclusive and adaptive, ethnic nationalism can be rigid and exclusionary, often leading to political tensions, particularly in multiethnic states.

The Rise of the Nation-State and the Impact of Nationalism

The 19th and 20th centuries saw nationalism reshape the world map, leading to both the creation of new states and the destruction of old empires.

The Unification of Germany and Italy – Nationalism was the driving force behind the creation of Germany (1871) and Italy (1861), where fragmented regions were brought together under a common national identity.

The Collapse of Multiethnic Empires – The Austro-Hungarian, Ottoman, and Russian Empires all disintegrated under nationalist pressures, as ethnic groups sought their own independent nations.

Decolonization and Anti-Colonial Nationalism – In the 20th century, nationalism inspired movements against European colonial rule in Africa, Asia, and Latin America, leading to the birth of new nations such as India (1947), Algeria (1962), and Ghana (1957).

Nationalism has played a liberating role in overthrowing colonial and imperial rule, but it has also fueled destructive wars and ethnic conflicts. The World Wars, the Rwandan Genocide, the Yugoslav Wars, and ongoing tensions in Ukraine all have roots in nationalist struggles.

Identity Politics: When Nationalism Meets Social Divisions

While nationalism focuses on the identity of the nation as a whole, identity politics is concerned with how specific social groups define themselves and seek political representation. It refers to the way in which race, ethnicity, gender, religion, and sexual orientation become central to political movements.

The Origins of Identity Politics

Though identity politics is often associated with contemporary debates, it has existed for centuries. The women's suffrage movement, the civil rights movement, and anti-colonial struggles were all forms of identity-based political action. These movements sought to challenge oppression and demand equal representation in a political system that marginalized certain groups.

However, in the late 20th and early 21st centuries, identity politics has become a dominant force in political discourse, particularly in liberal democracies.

The Debate Over Identity Politics

Supporters argue that identity-based political movements are necessary to correct historical injustices and ensure equal rights. They see movements like Black Lives Matter, LGBTQ+ rights, and Indigenous sovereignty as essential to democratizing power and giving marginalized groups a voice.

Critics, however, argue that identity politics can become divisive, creating an us-versus-them mentality that undermines social cohesion. Some believe it has contributed to the rise of populist backlash, as seen in movements like Donald Trump's America First campaign or Brexit, where voters rejected globalism in favor of a return to national identity.

In many ways, nationalism and identity politics are two sides of the same coin—both focus on group identity as the foundation of political action. The difference lies in who is included and who is excluded.

Nationalism, Identity, and the Future of Political Conflict

In the 21st century, nationalism and identity politics have become flashpoints of political conflict:

The Rise of Right-Wing Nationalism – In the US, Europe, and India, nationalist leaders have gained power by appealing to cultural identity and resisting globalization and immigration.

The Challenge of Multiculturalism – Many Western nations face tensions between national identity and the realities of multiethnic societies. France, for instance, has struggled to balance secular nationalism with its growing Muslim population.

Ethnic and Religious Conflicts – From Israel-Palestine to the Rohingya crisis in Myanmar, identity-based nationalism continues to drive violent conflicts.

As the world becomes more interconnected through globalization, migration, and digital communication, questions of who belongs, what defines a nation, and how political representation should be structured have become more pressing than ever.

Conclusion: Can Nationalism and Identity Politics Coexist?

Nationalism is not inherently bad, nor is identity politics inherently divisive. Both arise from a deep human need for belonging and recognition. The challenge is finding a balance between unity and diversity, between national identity and individual rights.

Can we build inclusive national identities that accommodate diverse cultures without erasing heritage?

Can identity politics promote equality without creating permanent social divisions?

Can globalism and nationalism coexist without constant conflict?

These are the defining questions of our time. The fate of democracy, peace, and social harmony may depend on how well we navigate them.

Imperialism and Colonialism
Historical Perspectives and Postcolonial Critiques

The story of imperialism and colonialism is the story of power—of expansion, domination, and resistance. It is the story of how empires stretched across continents, subjugating entire civilizations under foreign rule, and of how those subjected peoples fought for their independence, their identity, and their dignity. The legacy of this history is still present in the modern world, shaping global politics, economic inequality, and cultural narratives in profound ways.

Imperialism and colonialism are closely related but distinct. Imperialism refers to the policy or ideology of extending a nation's power and influence through military force, diplomacy, or economic control. Colonialism, on the other hand, is the practice of establishing and maintaining settlements or territories under the rule of a foreign power. While all colonialism is imperialistic in nature, not all imperialism results in direct colonial rule—economic domination and political interference can serve as softer, yet still coercive, forms of control.

The Rise of Empire: A Historical Overview

Empires have existed for as long as human civilization itself. The Roman Empire, the Persian Empire, the Mongol Empire, and the Chinese dynasties were among the great political forces that shaped history, governing vast, diverse populations under centralized rule. Yet, it was in the Age of Exploration (15th–17th centuries) that modern imperialism and colonialism began to take shape in the way that would define the world for centuries to come.

European Colonial Expansion: The Age of Empire

The late 15th century marked the beginning of European colonial expansion. Driven by a combination of economic ambition, religious zeal, and technological advancement, European powers sought to explore, conquer, and exploit new lands.

Spain and Portugal were the pioneers, launching maritime expeditions that led to the conquest of Latin America, the Caribbean, and parts of Africa and Asia.

Britain and France followed, establishing colonies in North America, the Caribbean, and later large portions of Africa and Asia.

The Netherlands, Belgium, and Germany also became significant colonial players, particularly in Southeast Asia and Africa.

The colonial project was justified through a mix of economic, religious, and pseudo-scientific arguments. The European powers claimed they were bringing civilization, Christianity, and progress to so-called "backward" societies. In reality, the colonial system functioned as a mechanism for economic exploitation, political domination, and cultural erasure.

The Machinery of Colonialism: How It Functioned

Colonial rule took many forms, from direct administration (as in British India or French Algeria) to indirect rule (as in the British protectorates in Africa, where local leaders were co-opted into the imperial system). Regardless of the form, colonialism functioned on several key mechanisms:

Economic Exploitation – Colonies were systematically stripped of their resources, which were extracted for the benefit of the imperial power.

The Atlantic slave trade saw millions of Africans forcibly transported to the Americas to work on plantations.

The British Raj in India drained vast amounts of wealth from the subcontinent through taxation and resource extraction.

Belgian rule in the Congo (1885–1960) was one of the most brutal examples, with forced labor and mass killings perpetrated for rubber and ivory.

Political Subjugation – Colonial administrations imposed foreign governance, often eliminating or severely restricting local self-rule.

Indigenous leaders were replaced by colonial officials.

Laws were crafted to serve imperial interests, often at the expense of local populations.

Cultural Suppression – Colonized peoples were forced to adopt the language, religion, and customs of their rulers.

Missionary education systems sought to indoctrinate indigenous populations into Western values.

Native languages, religions, and traditions were often banned or stigmatized.

Racial Hierarchies and Justifications – Colonization was frequently justified by racist ideologies that depicted non-European peoples as inferior.

The "White Man's Burden", a phrase coined by Rudyard Kipling, exemplified the belief that it was the duty of Westerners to "civilize" non-Europeans.

Social Darwinism was used to rationalize conquest, arguing that stronger races were destined to dominate weaker ones.

Resistance and Anti-Colonial Struggles

Despite the overwhelming power of colonial empires, resistance was constant. From armed revolts to intellectual and cultural movements, colonized peoples never accepted subjugation without a fight.

Early Resistance Movements

The Haitian Revolution (1791–1804) – Led by Toussaint Louverture, enslaved Africans in Haiti overthrew French rule and established the first black republic in the world.

The Indian Revolt of 1857 – Also known as the Sepoy Rebellion, this was one of the first major uprisings against British colonial rule in India.

The Zulu Resistance (1879) – Under Shaka Zulu and later

Cetshwayo, the Zulu kingdom fiercely resisted British and Boer expansion in southern Africa.

The 20th Century: Decolonization and the End of Empires

The collapse of colonial empires accelerated after World War II, when weakened European powers faced growing independence movements:

India and Pakistan gained independence in 1947, largely due to the efforts of leaders like Mahatma Gandhi and Jawaharlal Nehru.

African decolonization (1950s-70s) saw countries like Ghana (1957), Algeria (1962), and Kenya (1963) gain freedom after long struggles.

The Vietnam War (1955-1975) was, in part, a battle against continued colonial and neo-imperial influence.

While formal colonial rule ended in much of the world, its economic and political legacy remains, leading to the rise of postcolonial critiques.

Postcolonial Critiques: The Long Shadow of Empire

Even after independence, former colonies have struggled with political instability, economic dependency, and cultural fragmentation, often as a direct result of colonial policies.

Economic Dependency and Neocolonialism

Many newly independent nations found themselves trapped in a cycle of economic dependency on their former colonizers.

Multinational corporations and international financial institutions (e.g., the IMF and World Bank) have been accused of perpetuating economic imperialism.

Political Instability and Artificial Borders

The arbitrary borders drawn by colonial powers created nations with deep ethnic and religious divisions, leading to civil wars and political conflict (e.g., Rwanda, Sudan, Nigeria).

Cultural and Psychological Legacies

Frantz Fanon, a key postcolonial thinker, argued in The Wretched of the Earth that colonialism inflicted deep psychological wounds, leaving a legacy of inferiority complexes and identity crises.

Edward Said's concept of "Orientalism" highlighted how the West continues to depict non-Western societies as exotic, backward, or dangerous.

Conclusion: Imperialism's Lessons for the Present

Imperialism and colonialism are not just historical phenomena—their effects continue to shape the world today. The inequalities between the Global North and Global South, the struggles over identity and sovereignty, and the power dynamics in international relations all have roots in the colonial past.

The challenge for modern political philosophy is to understand and address these legacies:

How can former colonies achieve true economic independence?

How should nations deal with the cultural and social scars of colonialism?

Is globalization a new form of imperialism, or does it offer a path toward greater equity?

These questions remain open. The struggle against imperial domination may be a thing of the past, but the fight for justice in its aftermath is far from over.

POLITICAL PHILOSOPHY Summarized

War, Peace, and International Relations
Just War Theory, Realism vs. Liberalism in Global Politics, and International Law

Human history is, in many ways, the history of war. From ancient conflicts between city-states to the world wars of the 20th century and the ongoing geopolitical tensions of the 21st, war has shaped civilizations, redrawn borders, and transformed political orders. But alongside war has always been the pursuit of peace—whether through diplomacy, treaties, international law, or institutions aimed at preventing conflict. The study of war and peace is thus central to political philosophy and international relations, touching on deep moral, strategic, and legal questions.

Is war ever justified? If so, under what conditions? Are nations bound by moral constraints in warfare, or is power the only true law in global politics? How can states work together to maintain peace, and what are the limits of international cooperation? These are the questions that have defined just war theory, realism vs. liberalism in global politics, and international law—the three key pillars of this discussion.

Just War Theory: When Is War Morally Justifiable?

From the earliest times, thinkers have struggled with the question of whether war can ever be justified. Is war an inevitable reality of human existence, or can it be constrained by moral principles? The Just War tradition, which traces its roots to classical and medieval philosophy, attempts to provide a moral framework for war.

The Origins of Just War Theory

Just war theory can be traced back to Greek and Roman thought, but its most systematic early formulation comes from St. Augustine

(4th century CE) and Thomas Aquinas (13th century CE), both of whom sought to reconcile Christian ethics with the necessity of war. Aquinas developed three essential criteria for a war to be just:

Just Cause – War must be fought for a morally acceptable reason, such as self-defense or the protection of innocents.

Legitimate Authority – Only a recognized governing body has the right to declare war.

Right Intention – War must be fought for the right moral reasons, not for conquest or revenge.

Later, in the 17th century, Hugo Grotius, the Dutch philosopher known as the "father of international law," refined just war theory, arguing that nations had a right to defend themselves and that war should be limited by legal and moral constraints.

The Two Aspects of Just War: Jus ad Bellum and Jus in Bello

Modern just war theory is divided into two categories:

Jus ad Bellum (Justice Before War) – Determines when it is morally justifiable to go to war. Key principles include:

Self-defense – A nation may go to war to protect itself from aggression.

Last resort – War must be the final option after all diplomatic efforts fail.

Proportionality – The expected benefits of war must outweigh its harms.

Jus in Bello (Justice During War) – Defines how wars should be fought ethically. Key principles include:

Discrimination – Combatants must distinguish between military targets and civilians.

Proportionality – The level of force used must be proportionate to the military objective.

Prohibition of Unnecessary Suffering – The use of inhumane weapons or tactics is forbidden.

These principles have influenced modern laws of war, including the Geneva Conventions, which prohibit war crimes such as targeting civilians and torture.

However, just war theory has been criticized for being idealistic. Many argue that nations rarely follow ethical constraints when survival is at stake. This skepticism about moral constraints in war is a core principle of political realism.

Realism vs. Liberalism in Global Politics

The debate over war and peace is closely tied to broader theories of international relations, particularly the conflict between realism and liberalism. These two competing perspectives offer different visions of how states behave on the global stage and what drives international conflict and cooperation.

Realism: Power and National Interest

Realism is one of the oldest and most influential theories in international relations. Its fundamental assumption is that states exist in an anarchic international system, where there is no overarching authority to enforce laws or mediate disputes. In this world, power and national interest are the ultimate determinants of action.

Key Principles of Realism

The International System Is Anarchic – There is no global government to enforce order, meaning states must fend for themselves.

States Act in Their Own Self-Interest – Governments prioritize national security and power over morality or cooperation.

Might Makes Right – Military strength is the most reliable tool for securing a nation's interests.

Peace Is Temporary and Unstable – Conflicts arise naturally as nations compete for resources, security, and influence.

One of the most famous realist thinkers was Niccolò Machiavelli, who argued that rulers must prioritize power over morality. Similarly,

Thomas Hobbes described international relations as a state of perpetual conflict, where nations act like individuals in the "state of nature," always seeking advantage over others.

In the modern era, Hans Morgenthau and Kenneth Waltz further developed realism, emphasizing that war is a permanent feature of global politics. According to this view, diplomacy and international law are often mere illusions—useful when they serve national interests, but meaningless when power is at stake.

Liberalism: Cooperation and International Institutions

Liberalism, in contrast, argues that war is not inevitable and that states can cooperate through diplomacy, trade, and international institutions. Liberal theorists believe that law, democracy, and economic interdependence can create a more peaceful world.

Key Principles of Liberalism

Democracies Are Less Likely to Go to War – The Democratic Peace Theory suggests that democratic nations rarely fight each other.

Economic Interdependence Reduces Conflict – When states trade with each other, war becomes costly and undesirable.

International Institutions Promote Stability – Organizations like the United Nations, NATO, and the World Trade Organization help mediate disputes and prevent war.

Human Rights and Global Justice Matter – Morality and law should play a central role in foreign policy.

Liberalism gained prominence after World War II, leading to the creation of the United Nations, the European Union, and international human rights laws. Thinkers like Immanuel Kant argued for a global system of cooperation, believing that rational diplomacy could prevent war.

However, critics argue that liberalism is naïve—that states will always prioritize power over cooperation when faced with existential threats.

The Role of International Law in War and Peace

While realism suggests that power governs international politics, the rise of international law has sought to impose moral and legal constraints on war.

The Geneva Conventions (1864–1949) – Established rules for the treatment of prisoners, civilians, and wounded soldiers.

The United Nations Charter (1945) – Prohibits aggressive war and promotes diplomatic conflict resolution.

The International Criminal Court (ICC) – Prosecutes war crimes, genocide, and crimes against humanity.

While these laws have influenced global politics, enforcement remains difficult. Powerful nations can often ignore international law with little consequence, as seen in Russia's invasion of Ukraine, U.S. drone strikes, and China's territorial disputes in the South China Sea.

Conclusion: The Future of War and Peace

War and peace will always be central to political philosophy. Realists argue that conflict is inevitable, while liberals hold out hope for a world governed by law and cooperation. The balance between power and principle, war and diplomacy, national interest and international justice will continue to define global politics.

Can war ever truly be eradicated, or will the pursuit of peace always remain a fragile hope? The answer to this question will shape the future of civilization itself.

Feminist Political Thought

Wollstonecraft, de Beauvoir, and Modern Feminist Critiques of Political Structures

Throughout history, political philosophy has been overwhelmingly male-dominated, with ideas of governance, justice, and rights often framed from the perspective of men as the primary political actors. Women were largely excluded from formal political life—denied the right to vote, to hold office, or even to be recognized as full citizens. Feminist political thought emerged as a response to this exclusion, challenging the traditional philosophical and political frameworks that ignored or subordinated women.

Feminist political philosophy is not a single doctrine but a broad and evolving discourse that critiques how power, law, and political institutions have been structured in ways that disadvantage women. It asks fundamental questions: What is justice if half the population is excluded from its benefits? What does freedom mean when laws restrict women's autonomy? How does gender shape our understanding of power and political participation?

This chapter explores the foundational thinkers of feminist political thought—Mary Wollstonecraft and Simone de Beauvoir—as well as the evolution of feminist critiques of political structures, from early liberal feminism to contemporary debates on intersectionality, representation, and systemic oppression.

Mary Wollstonecraft: The Demand for Women's Political Rights

One of the first major figures in feminist political thought was Mary Wollstonecraft (1759-1797), a British philosopher and writer who is often considered the founding mother of modern feminism. Writing in the late 18th century, at a time when the Enlightenment was championing ideals of liberty, equality, and human rights, Wollstonecraft questioned why these principles did not extend to women.

A Vindication of the Rights of Woman (1792)

Wollstonecraft's most influential work, A Vindication of the Rights of Woman, was written in response to Jean-Jacques Rousseau's argument that women were naturally suited for domestic roles and that their education should be focused on making them obedient wives and mothers. Rejecting this notion, Wollstonecraft made a radical argument for her time:

Women are not naturally inferior to men but appear so because of a lack of education.

The exclusion of women from politics and education is unjust and hinders societal progress.

Women should have the same political rights as men, including access to education, property ownership, and political participation.

Her work was revolutionary because it placed women within the framework of liberal political thought, using Enlightenment ideals to argue for women's equality. Wollstonecraft believed that a just society could not exist if women were denied intellectual and political agency.

However, Wollstonecraft's feminism was still limited to a particular class of women—primarily white, educated, and middle-class. Her arguments focused on education and legal rights rather than broader structural critiques of patriarchy. Nonetheless, she laid the foundation for future feminist political thinkers who would push these ideas further.

Simone de Beauvoir: The Second Sex and the Social Construction of Gender

If Wollstonecraft set the stage for legal and political equality, it was

Simone de Beauvoir (1908-1986) who introduced a more philosophical and existential critique of women's oppression. A French existentialist and intellectual, de Beauvoir's groundbreaking work, The Second Sex (1949), remains one of the most influential feminist texts of all time.

"One is not born, but rather becomes, a woman."

This single sentence from The Second Sex encapsulates de Beauvoir's central argument: that gender is not simply a biological fact but a social and political construct. She distinguishes between:

Sex – The biological differences between men and women.

Gender – The cultural and social meanings assigned to these differences.

In patriarchal societies, women are defined not as autonomous individuals but in relation to men, as the "Other" to the male subject. Men represent the universal human experience, while women are cast as secondary, dependent, and limited to their reproductive roles.

De Beauvoir's Political Implications

De Beauvoir argued that women's oppression is not just a legal or economic issue but a deep existential condition—one that requires not only legal rights but also a radical transformation of society's values and expectations. Her work influenced later feminist movements, particularly radical feminism, which focused on challenging deeply ingrained patriarchal norms and power structures.

Waves of Feminist Political Thought

While Wollstonecraft and de Beauvoir were foundational, feminist political philosophy has continued to evolve, expanding its critiques and incorporating diverse perspectives. The history of feminism is often divided into three or four "waves", each with its distinct concerns and strategies.

First-Wave Feminism: Legal and Political Equality (19th – Early 20th Century)

The first wave focused on formal legal rights, particularly suffrage (the right to vote), property rights, and access to education.

Key Achievements:

The Seneca Falls Convention (1848) in the United States, where Elizabeth Cady Stanton and Lucretia Mott demanded women's right to vote.

The suffrage movements that led to voting rights for women in many Western countries (e.g., the 19th Amendment in the U.S., 1920; women's suffrage in the UK, 1918/1928).

Second-Wave Feminism: Expanding the Struggle (1960s–1980s)

Second-wave feminism moved beyond legal rights to address broader social, economic, and cultural inequalities.

Key Issues:

Workplace discrimination and wage inequality.

Reproductive rights (e.g., birth control, abortion rights).

The critique of domestic roles and the expectation that women should be confined to motherhood.

Thinkers like Betty Friedan (The Feminine Mystique) and bell hooks criticized the limitations of earlier feminism, calling for a broader fight against sexism in all aspects of life.

Third-Wave and Intersectional Feminism (1990s – Present)

Third-wave feminism challenged the homogeneity of earlier feminist movements, arguing that women's experiences are shaped by race, class, sexuality, and culture.

Intersectionality (coined by Kimberlé Crenshaw) examines how different forms of oppression (e.g., racism, sexism, classism) intersect.

Feminist critiques of capitalism (e.g., Nancy Fraser) argue that economic structures perpetuate gender inequality.

The rise of queer feminism challenges the gender binary itself.

Feminist Critiques of Political Structures

Feminist political thought extends beyond gender equality to critique power itself. Some key feminist critiques include:

The Male-Centered Nature of Politics – Traditional political thought assumes a universal "citizen" who is implicitly male.

The Public/Private Divide – Feminists argue that domestic labor and caregiving (traditionally assigned to women) are political issues, not just private matters.

Reproductive Rights and Bodily Autonomy – The control of women's bodies through law (e.g., abortion restrictions) is a form of political oppression.

Global Feminism – Western feminism often ignores the struggles of women in the Global South, who face different but interconnected challenges.

Conclusion: The Future of Feminist Political Thought

Feminist political philosophy has radically reshaped our understanding of rights, power, and justice. From Wollstonecraft's call for equal education to de Beauvoir's critique of gender norms, and from the suffragettes to modern intersectional feminism, the fight for equality continues.

The question remains: Can political systems originally designed to exclude women be transformed, or must entirely new systems be imagined? The answer to this will shape the next century of feminist political thought.

Multiculturalism and Political Pluralism

Theories of Integration, Diversity, and Cultural Identity

Few political topics in the modern world generate as much debate as multiculturalism. As societies grow increasingly diverse due to globalization, migration, and historical shifts in national identity, the question arises: How should political systems accommodate cultural differences? This is not merely an academic discussion—it has real-world consequences in policy, law, and social harmony.

At the heart of the debate is the tension between universal political principles and cultural particularism. Can a society maintain unity while embracing cultural diversity? Should the state promote integration, assimilation, or pluralism? Should minority groups be granted special rights, or should they be expected to conform to majority norms? These are the pressing questions that multiculturalism and political pluralism seek to answer.

To explore these issues, we will examine the philosophical foundations of multiculturalism, its political implications, and the critiques it faces.

The Meaning of Multiculturalism

Multiculturalism is not just a demographic fact—it is a political and philosophical stance that recognizes and seeks to accommodate cultural diversity within a society. While some view it as a celebration of diversity, others see it as a potential threat to national unity and social cohesion.

The term gained prominence in the late 20th century, especially in Western democracies that were grappling with large-scale immigration, indigenous rights, and postcolonial identities. At its core, multiculturalism argues that cultural differences should not only be tolerated but respected and protected through political and legal means.

Political theorists distinguish between three primary approaches to cultural diversity:

Assimilationism – Minority cultures are expected to adopt the dominant culture and conform to mainstream social norms.

Integrationism – Minority cultures are encouraged to retain their identities while also adopting aspects of the dominant culture.

Pluralism – Multiple cultural groups coexist with full recognition and equal status within a society.

Multiculturalism, in its strongest form, aligns with pluralism, advocating for the equal standing of all cultural traditions within a political framework.

Philosophical Foundations of Multiculturalism

Multicultural political thought is rooted in broader debates about liberalism, communitarianism, and justice. Some of its most influential defenders and critics come from these traditions.

Liberalism and the Politics of Recognition

Liberalism, particularly in its classical form, has traditionally emphasized individual rights over group identities. John Locke and John Stuart Mill argued that individuals should have the freedom to choose their own way of life, provided that they do not infringe upon the rights of others.

However, modern liberal theorists have grappled with the limits of individualism in diverse societies. Will Kymlicka, a leading advocate for multiculturalism, argues that culture is a primary context in which individuals form their identities and exercise their freedoms. In his book Multicultural Citizenship (1995), Kymlicka proposes that liberal democracies should recognize group-differentiated rights, including:

Language rights for minority and indigenous groups.

Cultural protections to maintain traditions without state interference.

Political representation for minority communities.

For Kymlicka, multiculturalism is not opposed to liberal democracy—it is a necessary extension of liberal principles to accommodate diverse cultural identities.

Communitarianism: The Value of Cultural Communities

While liberals emphasize individual rights, communitarians argue that identity is deeply rooted in social and cultural belonging. Charles Taylor and Michael Sandel emphasize that people do not exist in a vacuum—their values, beliefs, and sense of self are shaped by their cultural communities.

In his essay The Politics of Recognition, Taylor argues that societies must recognize cultural identities not just as a matter of tolerance but as a matter of justice. Without recognition, minority cultures risk marginalization and erasure.

However, this raises difficult questions: Should societies respect all cultural practices, even those that conflict with universal human rights? What happens when cultural preservation comes at the cost of individual freedoms, particularly for women, LGBTQ individuals, or dissenters within minority communities?

These tensions highlight the challenges of balancing group identity with individual autonomy.

Multiculturalism in Practice: Political and Legal Approaches

Multicultural policies vary widely across nations, reflecting different historical contexts, immigration patterns, and political philosophies.

Models of Multiculturalism

Liberal Multiculturalism (Canada, Australia, UK)

The state recognizes and funds cultural diversity through language protections, anti-discrimination laws, and multicultural education programs.

Canada's official bilingualism (English and French) and its recognition of indigenous rights are key examples.

Republican Integration (France, Turkey, Some Parts of Europe)

National identity is prioritized over cultural differences.

France's laïcité (strict secularism) restricts religious expression (e.g., bans on headscarves in schools) in an effort to promote a shared national culture.

Ethnic Nationalism and Exclusionary Policies (Japan, China, Some European Movements)

Some countries define citizenship in ethnic or cultural terms, making full integration difficult for minority groups.

The Challenge of Religious and Ethnic Pluralism

Religious and ethnic diversity often complicates multicultural policies.

Religious exemptions (e.g., allowing Sikhs to wear turbans in police uniforms) raise questions about legal equality.

Ethnic enclaves can create parallel societies, leading to fears of segregation rather than integration.

The burqa ban debates in Europe illustrate these tensions: some view bans on Islamic dress as defense of secular values, while others see them as a violation of religious freedom.

Critiques of Multiculturalism

While multiculturalism aims to promote inclusion and diversity, it has been subject to significant criticism from both the right and the left.

Conservative and Nationalist Critiques

Multiculturalism weakens national identity and creates social fragmentation.

Promoting separate cultural identities undermines social cohesion and creates "parallel societies" with conflicting values.

Right-wing populists argue that multicultural policies favor minorities at the expense of the majority, particularly in immigration debates.

Leftist and Feminist Critiques

Some leftists argue that multiculturalism is a neoliberal strategy that ignores economic inequalities—it promotes cultural recognition without addressing material disparities.

Feminists critique multiculturalism for protecting patriarchal traditions, such as honor killings, arranged marriages, and restrictive gender norms.

Ayaan Hirsi Ali argues that cultural relativism often excuses human rights abuses in the name of diversity.

These critiques demonstrate that multiculturalism is not a universally accepted political ideal—it is a contested concept with deep philosophical and practical challenges.

Conclusion: The Future of Political Pluralism

Multiculturalism is a defining issue of the 21st century, shaping debates on immigration, citizenship, education, and national identity. The question is not whether societies will be diverse—they already are—but rather how to govern diversity fairly.

Should political systems encourage full integration into a common national culture, or should they protect and sustain multiple cultural identities? Can democracy thrive in societies with deep cultural divisions, or does political unity require some level of assimilation?

The answers to these questions will shape the political landscapes of nations, communities, and global governance for decades to come.

Environmental Political Philosophy

The Politics of Climate Change, Sustainability, and Eco-Philosophy

Few challenges in contemporary political philosophy are as urgent as the environmental crisis. Climate change, deforestation, biodiversity loss, and pollution threaten not only the health of ecosystems but the very foundations of human civilization. Yet, despite the overwhelming scientific consensus on environmental degradation, political responses remain fragmented, slow, and often insufficient.

This raises profound philosophical and political questions: What is the moral status of nature? Do future generations have rights? Should we prioritize economic growth over environmental sustainability? How should political institutions respond to the ecological crisis?

Environmental political philosophy is a relatively new but rapidly growing field, drawing from ethics, political theory, economics, and law to address these fundamental questions. It critiques traditional political frameworks that prioritize human interests over ecological health and seeks to construct new models of governance that recognize the interdependence of human and natural systems.

This chapter explores the political dimensions of climate change, sustainability, and eco-philosophy, examining the philosophical foundations of environmental thought, the challenges of environmental justice, and the role of states, markets, and global institutions in addressing the crisis.

The Philosophical Foundations of Environmental Political Thought

Historically, Western political philosophy has been anthropocentric—placing human beings at the center of moral and political concern. Nature was often seen as a resource to be exploited, with little intrinsic value beyond its usefulness to human society.

This view is evident in thinkers like John Locke, who argued that land and nature only gained value when cultivated by human labor. Similarly, Immanuel Kant maintained that moral worth applied only to rational beings, leaving animals and ecosystems outside the sphere of ethical concern.

However, modern environmental philosophy challenges this anthropocentrism, arguing for a broader ethical framework that includes the rights of nature, ecological balance, and intergenerational justice.

Deep Ecology vs. Shallow Ecology

One of the key divisions in environmental philosophy is between deep ecology and shallow ecology.

Shallow Ecology focuses on human-centered environmentalism, seeking to preserve nature primarily for its benefits to people—clean air, stable climate, and economic resources.

Deep Ecology, a term coined by Arne Naess, argues that nature has intrinsic value, independent of its usefulness to humans. It promotes a radical shift in thinking, advocating for policies that prioritize ecological balance over economic growth.

This distinction shapes political debates: Should we protect forests because they store carbon and provide resources, or because they have an inherent right to exist? Should policies focus on managing environmental harm, or fundamentally restructuring society's relationship with nature?

The Politics of Climate Change

Climate change is perhaps the most pressing issue in environmental political philosophy. Scientific evidence is clear: human activities, particularly the burning of fossil fuels, are driving global temperatures higher, leading to extreme weather, rising sea levels, and ecosystem collapse.

However, political responses to climate change remain inadequate, hindered by short-term economic interests, political inertia, and the power of fossil fuel industries. This has led to intense debates about the responsibility of governments, corporations, and individuals in addressing the crisis.

The Tragedy of the Commons

A key concept in environmental political thought is the tragedy of the commons, first articulated by Garrett Hardin in 1968. Hardin described how shared resources (like the atmosphere, oceans, or forests) tend to be overexploited because individuals and nations prioritize their own short-term gains over long-term sustainability.

This explains why countries struggle to cooperate on climate action—reducing emissions is costly, and no single nation wants to bear the burden while others continue polluting. This leads to free-riding, where some nations benefit from the environmental efforts of others without making sacrifices themselves.

Climate Justice: Who Bears the Burden?

Climate change is not just an environmental problem—it is also a political and ethical issue of justice. The countries that have contributed the least to climate change (mainly in the Global South) are suffering the most from its effects, while wealthy industrialized nations—historically the largest polluters—continue to benefit from fossil-fueled economies.

This raises critical questions:

Who is responsible for addressing climate change?

Should wealthy nations pay "climate reparations" to poorer countries suffering from environmental destruction?

How can developing nations achieve economic growth without following the same polluting path as industrialized countries?

These questions fuel the debate between global North and South, with developing nations arguing that they should not be forced to bear the economic costs of a problem they did not create.

Sustainability: Can Politics Balance Growth and Ecology?

Another major concern in environmental political philosophy is sustainability—how societies can meet the needs of the present without compromising the ability of future generations to meet their own needs.

However, this goal is often at odds with dominant economic models, which prioritize growth, consumption, and short-term profits. Capitalism, in particular, is built on the assumption of endless expansion, leading critics to argue that a sustainable future requires rethinking economic systems altogether.

Green Politics and Ecological Democracy

One response to environmental challenges has been the rise of Green Politics, a movement that integrates environmentalism into political governance. Green parties and activists advocate for:

Renewable energy and carbon taxes to reduce fossil fuel dependence.

Environmental regulations and corporate accountability.

Participatory democracy, where citizens have a greater say in environmental policies affecting their communities.

Thinkers like Murray Bookchin have called for ecological democracy, arguing that hierarchical political and economic systems are the root of environmental destruction and that sustainable societies must be built on decentralized, community-driven governance.

Eco-Socialism, Eco-Fascism, and the Politics of Environmentalism

Environmentalism is not politically neutral—it has been interpreted in radically different ways across the ideological spectrum.

Eco-Socialists argue that capitalism is incompatible with ecological sustainability. Figures like André Gorz and Naomi Klein call for an economic system that prioritizes people and the planet over corporate profits.

Eco-Fascists, in contrast, promote a reactionary, nationalist version of environmentalism, often blending ecological concerns with anti-immigrant, racist, and authoritarian ideologies.

Neoliberal Environmentalism, dominant in mainstream politics, seeks market-based solutions (e.g., carbon trading, green technology investment) without challenging existing economic structures.

These competing visions demonstrate that environmentalism is not a single movement—it is a battleground for different political ideologies.

The Role of Global Governance

Since climate change and environmental destruction do not respect national borders, global cooperation is essential. International efforts like:

The Paris Agreement (2015) – A global climate treaty aiming to limit temperature rise to 1.5°C.

The United Nations Sustainable Development Goals (SDGs) – A set of international goals for environmental and social sustainability.

The Intergovernmental Panel on Climate Change (IPCC) – A scientific body advising governments on climate action.

However, global environmental governance is weakened by political resistance, corporate lobbying, and national self-interest.

Conclusion: The Future of Environmental Political Thought

Environmental political philosophy forces us to rethink our relationship with nature, our economic models, and our political institutions. The climate crisis is not just a scientific or technological challenge—it is a deeply political issue that raises fundamental questions about justice, responsibility, and the limits of human power.

Will we restructure our societies in time to prevent catastrophe, or will political inertia lead us toward ecological collapse? The decisions made in the coming decades will shape the future of both human civilization and the natural world itself.

Technology and Political Power

Surveillance, Digital Authoritarianism, and the Politics of Artificial Intelligence

Technology has always been intertwined with political power. From the printing press to the internet, innovations in communication and information technology have shaped how societies are governed, how authority is enforced, and how resistance emerges. In the 21st century, however, the relationship between technology and political power has become more complex and pervasive than ever before.

The rise of digital surveillance, artificial intelligence (AI), and data-driven governance has given states and corporations unprecedented tools to monitor, influence, and control populations. Some argue that these technologies can enhance democracy, making governments more efficient, transparent, and responsive. Others warn that we are entering an era of digital authoritarianism, where power is consolidated in the hands of a few, and citizens are subjected to ever-expanding forms of surveillance and control.

This chapter explores the political implications of modern technology, focusing on surveillance, the rise of digital authoritarianism, and the ethical dilemmas posed by artificial intelligence.

The Rise of the Surveillance State

The modern state has always sought ways to gather information about its citizens. From census data to intelligence agencies, governments have historically used surveillance to maintain order, enforce laws, and protect national security. However, the digital revolution has transformed the scale and sophistication of surveillance.

Mass Surveillance in the Digital Age

Traditional surveillance involved physical monitoring, phone tapping, and intelligence gathering through human informants. Today, however, mass surveillance is automated, data-driven, and nearly omnipresent. Governments and corporations collect vast amounts of personal data through:

Smartphones and GPS tracking – Governments can monitor the real-time locations of millions of people.

Social media and online activity – Digital footprints reveal political views, personal habits, and social connections.

Facial recognition and biometrics – Security cameras equipped with AI can identify individuals in public spaces.

Big data analytics and predictive policing – Algorithms process massive datasets to predict and prevent crimes, often raising ethical concerns about bias and discrimination.

Perhaps the most well-known example of mass surveillance was exposed by Edward Snowden in 2013, when he revealed that the U.S. National Security Agency (NSA) was conducting global surveillance programs, collecting data from millions of civilians and even spying on world leaders. These revelations sparked global debates about privacy, government overreach, and the role of technology in governance.

The Trade-Off Between Security and Privacy

Defenders of surveillance argue that it is necessary for national security—to prevent terrorism, cybercrime, and foreign espionage. However, critics warn that mass surveillance erodes civil liberties, creating a society where individuals are constantly watched and afraid to express dissent.

This raises fundamental political questions:

Does increased security justify the loss of privacy?

Who controls surveillance data, and how can abuse be prevented?

What mechanisms exist to ensure government accountability in the digital age?

Many liberal democracies attempt to balance security with individual rights through oversight institutions, legal frameworks, and independent watchdogs. However, in authoritarian regimes, surveillance is often used to crush dissent, monitor political opponents, and enforce ideological conformity.

Digital Authoritarianism: A New Form of Political Control

While technology can be a force for democratization—empowering people through access to information and communication—it can also be weaponized by authoritarian regimes to strengthen their grip on power.

Digital authoritarianism refers to the use of technology to surveil, manipulate, and control populations, often in ways that undermine human rights and democratic governance. Some of its key features include:

The Chinese Model: The Rise of the Surveillance State

China provides the most advanced and sophisticated example of digital authoritarianism. Through its Social Credit System, the government tracks citizens' behaviors—both online and offline—and assigns them scores based on their "trustworthiness." These scores influence:

Employment opportunities

Access to loans and travel

Social privileges

Additionally, China has developed one of the world's most extensive facial recognition networks, enabling the government to track individuals in real time. Protesters, journalists, and dissidents are often identified and silenced before they can challenge the system.

China's Great Firewall also tightly controls internet access, restricting information, censoring dissent, and promoting state-approved narratives. This model has inspired other regimes, with countries like Russia, Iran, and Saudi Arabia adopting similar internet controls to suppress opposition.

The Global Spread of Digital Authoritarianism

While China's system is the most comprehensive, elements of digital authoritarianism can be seen worldwide.

Russia has been accused of spreading disinformation and controlling online narratives to maintain political stability.

India has implemented internet blackouts in politically sensitive regions to suppress protests and dissent.

The United States and Europe have engaged in mass surveillance under the guise of national security.

These cases demonstrate that digital authoritarianism is not limited to traditionally authoritarian states—even democracies are struggling with the implications of increasing technological control.

Artificial Intelligence and Political Power

Artificial intelligence (AI) is one of the most disruptive political technologies of our time. While AI offers opportunities for efficiency, automation, and problem-solving, it also raises serious ethical and political concerns.

AI in Governance: Efficiency or Oppression?

Governments are increasingly using AI to:

Automate decision-making in law enforcement, welfare, and immigration.

Predict and prevent crimes through AI-driven policing.

Influence public opinion through personalized propaganda and targeted advertisements.

While AI can improve government efficiency, it also poses risks of bias, discrimination, and a lack of accountability. Who is responsible when an AI system makes an unfair or harmful decision?

The Threat of Autonomous Weapons

One of the most alarming developments in AI is the rise of autonomous weapons, or "killer robots," that can select and engage targets without human intervention. These technologies raise serious ethical concerns:

Who is accountable for civilian casualties?

Can AI be programmed to follow ethical rules in warfare?

Could AI-driven war escalate conflicts beyond human control?

Despite calls for an international ban on autonomous weapons, many countries, including the U.S., China, and Russia, continue to develop them.

Conclusion: The Future of Political Power in the Digital Age

The intersection of technology and political power presents both opportunities and threats. While technology can enhance democracy, transparency, and governance, it also provides tools for authoritarian control, mass surveillance, and AI-driven oppression.

Key Questions for the Future:

How can we regulate digital surveillance without compromising security?

What mechanisms can prevent the abuse of AI in governance?

Should there be international treaties against digital authoritarianism and autonomous weapons?

How do we ensure that emerging technologies serve democracy

rather than undermine it?

The answers to these questions will determine whether the digital revolution leads to a more just and open world—or a future of unprecedented technological control and oppression.

Future of Political Philosophy

Emerging Issues, Post-Humanist Politics, and the Role of Philosophy in an Uncertain World

Political philosophy has always evolved alongside the shifting realities of human civilization. From Plato's ideal state to Marx's critique of capitalism, from Hobbes' Leviathan to the modern dilemmas of surveillance and artificial intelligence, political thought has responded to the challenges of its time. But what happens when the world changes so radically that traditional political categories no longer apply?

We are entering an era where technology, climate change, globalization, and cultural transformations are reshaping the very foundations of political life. The nation-state, the concept of citizenship, and even the nature of governance itself are being challenged in ways that political theorists of the past could hardly have imagined. This demands a new kind of political philosophy—one that does not merely refine old ideas but asks new questions about the nature of power, rights, and justice in a rapidly changing world.

This chapter explores some of the emerging frontiers of political thought, from the challenges posed by post-humanism and artificial intelligence to the future of democracy, globalization, and the very idea of political authority.

The Crisis of Traditional Political Categories

For much of history, political philosophy has been built on

assumptions about the human condition: that individuals exist within nation-states, that they are biological beings with physical needs, and that politics is fundamentally about managing resources, power, and conflicts within human communities. But in the 21st century, each of these assumptions is being questioned.

The Nation-State in Decline?

The nation-state has been the dominant political structure for centuries, but globalization, climate change, and digital technology are eroding its power. Consider the following:

Multinational corporations—Amazon, Google, Facebook—wield economic and political power greater than many governments.

Cryptocurrencies challenge the state's traditional monopoly on money.

Climate refugees are creating border crises that nation-states struggle to address.

Global governance institutions (e.g., the United Nations, the World Economic Forum) are growing in influence, raising questions about sovereignty and democracy.

As power shifts from governments to global networks, we must ask: Will the nation-state survive? Or are we moving toward a post-national world?

Some philosophers argue that nation-states are outdated—that in a world of transnational problems, we need global governance. Others warn that a world without nation-states could become a corporate dystopia, where decisions are made by unelected technocrats rather than democratic institutions.

The Death of the Human Citizen?

Traditional political philosophy assumes that political subjects are human beings. But what happens when artificial intelligence, biotechnology, and robotics challenge our understanding of what it means to be a political agent?

Artificial intelligence already makes decisions that affect millions of lives. Should AI have legal or political status? If an AI algorithm controls financial markets or social policy, is it a political actor?

Genetic engineering and cybernetic enhancement may soon allow people to modify their biology in radical ways. If a person uploads their consciousness to a machine, do they retain legal rights? Are they still a citizen?

Non-human animals and ecosystems are increasingly recognized as having moral significance. Should they also have political representation? Some environmental thinkers argue for a "Parliament of Things", where nature itself has political rights.

These questions force us to rethink the very definition of political participation and citizenship. Are we moving toward a post-human political order?

The Role of Technology in Shaping the Future of Politics

Artificial Intelligence and Automated Governance

One of the most profound challenges facing political philosophy is the rise of AI-driven governance. Today, algorithms:

Determine parole sentences in some legal systems.

Set interest rates and influence financial markets.

Moderate political speech on social media platforms.

The argument in favor of AI governance is efficiency—machines can make rational, unbiased decisions faster than humans. But critics warn of opaque algorithms, loss of accountability, and the erosion of democracy.

If governments increasingly rely on AI to make policy decisions, does this weaken democratic legitimacy? And if AI can make better decisions than elected officials, should we replace politicians with machines?

These are no longer science fiction questions. In China, AI-driven surveillance and automated law enforcement are already shaping the daily lives of citizens. This forces us to ask:

Is democracy compatible with AI-driven decision-making?

Who should be responsible when an AI system makes a political mistake?

How do we ensure that AI governance respects human rights and ethics?

Post-Democracy: What Comes After Representative Government?

Liberal democracy has long been considered the pinnacle of political evolution. But today, faith in democracy is declining worldwide. Voter turnout is low, trust in governments is eroding, and populism and authoritarianism are on the rise.

Some argue that democracy itself is outdated. Political theorists like Jason Brennan advocate for epistocracy—a system where only the most knowledgeable citizens vote. Others propose liquid democracy, where votes are delegated to experts in different fields.

The real question is: Can democracy evolve to meet the challenges of the 21st century, or will it be replaced by new forms of governance?

Climate Change and the End of Politics as We Know It

Perhaps the most existential challenge to political philosophy is climate change. Rising temperatures, extreme weather, and resource scarcity could make many political theories obsolete.

What happens to political rights when survival itself is at risk?

Should governments suspend democracy to enact drastic environmental policies?

Who has the right to relocate climate refugees when entire nations disappear under rising seas?

These questions demand an urgent rethinking of political philosophy. Some argue that authoritarian environmentalism—where governments take drastic action to save the planet—is necessary. Others believe that only radical democracy and grassroots movements can address climate change effectively.

Either way, one thing is clear: traditional politics will not survive the ecological crisis unchanged.

Conclusion: The Role of Political Philosophy in an Uncertain World

With so many radical transformations on the horizon, what role does political philosophy play? Some argue that philosophy has become irrelevant—that technology and markets now dictate the course of history. But this view is dangerously short-sighted.

Philosophy remains essential because it provides:

Moral clarity—guiding discussions about rights, justice, and human dignity.

Conceptual frameworks—helping us understand new political realities.

Critical reflection—challenging the assumptions behind policies and institutions.

Political philosophy may not provide definitive answers, but it helps us ask better questions—questions that shape the laws, values, and institutions of the future.

Will the future of political thought be dictated by algorithms and economic forces, or will humanity take control of its own destiny? The answer depends on our ability to think critically, ethically, and politically about the world that is emerging before us.

In this sense, political philosophy is not just an academic exercise—it is a necessity for the survival of free and just societies.

Conclusion: Why Political Philosophy Matters

A Synthesis of Key Ideas and Their Relevance to Modern Life

Political philosophy is not a relic of the past, nor is it merely an abstract academic pursuit. It is the foundation upon which societies are built, the intellectual framework through which we understand governance, power, justice, and rights. Whether one realizes it or not, political philosophy shapes every aspect of our daily lives—from the laws that govern us to the economic systems that structure our interactions, from the moral principles that inform justice to the very idea of what it means to be free.

In this book, we have journeyed through the fundamental concepts, historical developments, and pressing modern challenges of political philosophy. We have examined the nature of the state, the debates over justice and liberty, the conflicts between different economic and political systems, and the emerging challenges posed by technology, globalization, and climate change. As we conclude this exploration, one question remains: Why does political philosophy still matter today?

The answer is simple yet profound: because political philosophy is the lens through which we navigate the complexities of the modern world. Without it, we are blind to the forces shaping our societies, unable to critically assess the legitimacy of power, and incapable of envisioning a better future. In this final chapter, we will reflect on the key insights from our exploration and discuss the enduring significance of political philosophy in contemporary life.

The Enduring Questions of Political Philosophy

Despite the vast differences between ancient Athens, medieval

Europe, and the digital age, the fundamental questions of political philosophy remain strikingly consistent:

What is justice? Is it best understood through Plato's ideal state, Rawls' veil of ignorance, or Nozick's libertarian minimalism?

What is the role of the state? Should it be Leviathan, the night-watchman, or an instrument of collective self-determination?

What are the limits of freedom? Is liberty best defined negatively (as freedom from interference) or positively (as self-actualization and empowerment)?

How should wealth and power be distributed? Does Marx's class struggle still define economic life, or have new forms of inequality emerged in the 21st century?

What makes authority legitimate? Is democracy the final form of governance, or does it have fundamental flaws that call for new political models?

These questions are not merely intellectual exercises—they are the core dilemmas that shape real-world politics. The tensions between liberty and security, equality and meritocracy, democracy and efficiency are present in every society. Political philosophy provides the conceptual tools to navigate these tensions and articulate solutions that align with our values.

Political Philosophy in the 21st Century: Key Challenges

1. Democracy in Crisis

Throughout this book, we have examined both the virtues and weaknesses of democracy. While democratic governance is often championed as the best system for securing freedom and justice, contemporary events reveal deep challenges:

Rising populism, fueled by economic frustration and cultural divides, has led to a crisis of confidence in democratic institutions.

Misinformation and social media manipulation undermine informed decision-making and encourage political polarization.

Low voter participation suggests that many citizens feel disillusioned, powerless, or disengaged.

Does this mean democracy has failed? Not necessarily. But it does mean that we must rethink how democracy functions in the modern world. The theories of Rousseau, Mill, and Schumpeter remain as relevant as ever, offering insights into how democratic legitimacy, citizen participation, and governance structures can be improved.

2. Globalization and the Decline of the Nation-State

The nation-state has been the dominant political unit for centuries, but as we discussed in earlier chapters, it is now under pressure from global economic forces, international institutions, transnational corporations, and climate change.

If multinational corporations have more influence than elected governments, who holds power?

If climate refugees cross borders in search of survival, who is responsible for their rights and protections?

If artificial intelligence and digital surveillance shape public opinion, who controls political discourse?

These are new challenges that traditional political theories do not fully address, forcing us to develop new frameworks for understanding power, sovereignty, and governance in a post-national world.

3. Technology, Artificial Intelligence, and the Future of Politics

One of the most pressing frontiers of political philosophy is the impact of technology on power, autonomy, and democracy.

AI-driven governance raises questions about accountability, bias, and the role of human decision-making.

Surveillance technologies challenge our assumptions about privacy and the limits of state power.

Digital authoritarianism demonstrates how technology can be

used to control, manipulate, and suppress dissent.

Political philosophy must grapple with these new realities. As we move forward, we must decide whether we will allow technology to dictate the future of politics, or whether we will use political philosophy to shape technology in alignment with democratic values.

The Role of Political Philosophy in Shaping the Future

If political philosophy has taught us anything, it is that the future is not predetermined. Societies change, ideologies rise and fall, and revolutions—both intellectual and political—reshape the world. What remains constant is the need for critical thought, ethical reflection, and political imagination.

1. Thinking Critically About Power

One of the greatest contributions of political philosophy is its ability to challenge assumptions about power. Whether questioning the legitimacy of kings, the justifications of capitalism, or the ethics of surveillance, political philosophy forces us to ask:

Who benefits from the existing system?

Who is excluded or oppressed?

What alternative forms of governance are possible?

Without critical inquiry, power goes unchecked, injustice becomes normalized, and democracy decays into complacency and manipulation. Political philosophy reminds us that no system is inevitable or beyond scrutiny.

2. Bridging Ideological Divides

In an era of extreme political polarization, philosophy offers a space for dialogue. By engaging with thinkers from opposing traditions—liberalism, conservatism, socialism, libertarianism—we develop a deeper understanding of the trade-offs inherent in political decisions.

Political philosophy does not demand that we all agree—it demands that we think deeply and argue honestly.

3. Envisioning a Better Future

Finally, political philosophy is not just about critiquing the present—it is about imagining new possibilities. Every political transformation—from the abolition of slavery to the rise of democracy, from the feminist movement to the fight for digital rights—began as a philosophical idea before becoming reality.

If we want a world that is more just, more free, and more sustainable, we need political philosophy to provide the framework for creating it.

Final Thoughts: Why Political Philosophy Matters

As we stand on the precipice of a new era—marked by technological upheaval, environmental crisis, and shifting political landscapes—the need for deep, thoughtful political philosophy has never been greater.

We may not have all the answers, but as long as we continue to ask the right questions—about justice, power, freedom, and the role of the state—political philosophy will remain one of the most vital disciplines in shaping the world of tomorrow.

In the end, political philosophy matters because politics matters—and politics matters because people matter. If we care about the kind of world we are creating, then we must take political philosophy seriously—not just as an academic pursuit, but as a practical tool for making society more just, more free, and more humane.

Further Reading

For those who wish to explore political philosophy in greater depth, the following list provides a structured path through foundational texts, major theoretical debates, and contemporary discussions. These works range from classical treatises to modern analyses, covering themes such as justice, democracy, power, rights, and governance.

Classical Political Philosophy
Plato – The Republic (c. 375 BCE)
A cornerstone of Western political thought, The Republic explores justice, the ideal state, and the role of the philosopher-king. Plato's vision of a hierarchical and well-ordered society continues to influence political theory.

Aristotle – Politics (c. 350 BCE)
Aristotle provides a pragmatic and empirical approach to governance, categorizing different political systems and emphasizing the importance of virtue and civic participation in a just society.

Cicero – On the Republic and On the Laws (c. 54 BCE)
An essential Roman contribution to political philosophy, Cicero defends republicanism and the rule of law, laying the groundwork for later discussions on constitutionalism and mixed government.

Medieval and Renaissance Political Thought
Augustine – The City of God (c. 426 CE)
Augustine contrasts the "City of Man" (earthly politics) with the "City of God," arguing that divine authority transcends human political institutions, influencing Christian political thought for centuries.

Thomas Aquinas – Summa Theologica (Selections, 13th Century)
A synthesis of Christian theology and Aristotelian philosophy,

Aquinas' work defends the idea of natural law, emphasizing the moral foundations of government and law.

Niccolò Machiavelli – The Prince (1513)

A groundbreaking realist text, The Prince examines power, strategy, and statecraft, arguing that rulers must sometimes employ ruthless tactics to maintain political stability.

Niccolò Machiavelli – Discourses on Livy (c. 1517)

Unlike The Prince, this work champions republicanism and civic virtue, providing an important counterpoint to his more authoritarian arguments.

Social Contract Theory and Early Modern Political Philosophy

Thomas Hobbes – Leviathan (1651)

Hobbes presents a bleak view of human nature, arguing that a strong, absolute government is necessary to prevent chaos and maintain social order.

John Locke – Two Treatises of Government (1689)

Locke lays the foundation for modern liberal democracy, advocating for natural rights, limited government, and the right to revolution against tyranny.

Jean-Jacques Rousseau – The Social Contract (1762)

Rousseau presents a radical democratic vision in which sovereignty lies with the people and governance must reflect the "general will."

The Enlightenment and Revolutionary Political Thought

Montesquieu – The Spirit of the Laws (1748)

A foundational text advocating for the separation of powers, which greatly influenced modern democratic constitutions.

Edmund Burke – Reflections on the Revolution in France (1790)

Burke provides a passionate defense of tradition, gradual change, and conservative principles in response to the radicalism of the French Revolution.

Thomas Paine – Common Sense (1776) & The Rights of Man (1791)

A powerful case for democracy, individual rights, and revolution against tyranny, influencing both American and French revolutionary thought.

Immanuel Kant – Perpetual Peace: A Philosophical Sketch (1795)

An early argument for international cooperation and a vision of peace through legal and institutional structures.

Utilitarianism and Classical Liberalism

Jeremy Bentham – An Introduction to the Principles of Morals and Legislation (1789)

The founding text of utilitarianism, arguing that government should maximize happiness for the greatest number.

John Stuart Mill – On Liberty (1859) & Considerations on Representative Government (1861)

A defense of individual freedom, free speech, and representative democracy, essential to modern liberal thought.

Marxism and Critiques of Capitalism

Karl Marx and Friedrich Engels – The Communist Manifesto (1848)

A call for proletarian revolution against capitalist exploitation, foundational to socialist and communist movements.

Karl Marx – Capital: Critique of Political Economy (1867)

A comprehensive critique of capitalism, labor exploitation, and economic systems, still widely studied in political economy.

20th and 21st Century Political Thought

Max Weber – Politics as a Vocation (1919)

An essential work on political authority, bureaucracy, and the nature of power in modern societies.

Carl Schmitt – The Concept of the Political (1932)

A critique of liberal democracy, arguing that politics is defined by the distinction between friends and enemies.

John Rawls – A Theory of Justice (1971)

One of the most important works in modern political philosophy, advocating for justice as fairness through principles of liberty and equality.

Robert Nozick – Anarchy, State, and Utopia (1974)

A libertarian response to Rawls, defending a minimal state and strong property rights.

Hannah Arendt – The Origins of Totalitarianism (1951)

A seminal analysis of the rise of totalitarian regimes, focusing on Nazi Germany and Stalinist Russia.

Michel Foucault – Discipline and Punish (1975) & The History of Sexuality (1976-84)

A critique of power structures, institutions, and the ways in which politics influences knowledge and identity.

Frantz Fanon – The Wretched of the Earth (1961)

A foundational work in postcolonial theory, analyzing the psychological and political effects of colonialism.

Simone de Beauvoir – The Second Sex (1949)

A key feminist critique of political and social structures that perpetuate gender inequality.

Jürgen Habermas – The Structural Transformation of the Public Sphere (1962)

Analyzes how communication and deliberation shape democracy and political legitimacy.

Contemporary Political Thought

Martha Nussbaum – Political Emotions: Why Love Matters for

Justice (2013)

A compelling argument on how emotions shape democracy and social justice.

Chantal Mouffe – The Democratic Paradox (2000)

A critique of liberal democracy and an argument for embracing political conflict and pluralism.

Francis Fukuyama – The End of History and the Last Man (1992)

Argues that liberal democracy represents the final stage of political evolution, though widely debated.

Slavoj Žižek – The Sublime Object of Ideology (1989)

A psychoanalytic critique of ideology, capitalism, and political discourse.

Wendy Brown – Undoing the Demos: Neoliberalism's Stealth Revolution (2015)

A critical examination of how neoliberalism transforms democratic institutions.

Epilogue

The Never-Ending Debate

Political philosophy is not a subject you learn once and set aside, like a dusty old book on a shelf. It is the intellectual lifeblood of civilization, an ongoing battle of ideas that determines the fate of nations, the structure of societies, and the freedoms—or chains—of individuals.

From the earliest city-states of Athens to the digitized world of today, the fundamental questions have remained the same: Who should rule? What is justice? What are the limits of freedom? These are not just theoretical musings of long-dead philosophers. They are the very struggles that continue to shape our world in real-time—on the streets, in parliaments, in courtrooms, and behind closed doors where power is wielded.

As we stand at the crossroads of an uncertain future, the questions have only grown more urgent. The rise of artificial intelligence, mass surveillance, global inequality, and political polarization challenges the very foundations of governance as we know it. Will the democratic experiment survive the strains of misinformation and division? Will the battle between freedom and security tilt towards authoritarianism? Can societies adapt to economic and technological revolutions without collapsing into chaos?

These questions have no final answers—only evolving arguments. Each generation finds itself forced to reinterpret the wisdom of the past in light of new realities. And now, the responsibility falls on you, the reader. To engage, to question, to think critically. To recognize that politics is not something that happens "out there"—it is woven into every aspect of life, shaping the freedoms you enjoy, the structures you obey, and the rights you defend.

So, what will you do with this knowledge? Will you stand by and watch as history unfolds, or will you take part in the debates that will define the future? One thing is certain: political philosophy is far from over. It is alive, pulsing, shifting—waiting for the next great thinker to step forward.

Perhaps that thinker is you.

THE END

Join The SUMIT Community

The journey of understanding doesn't end with a single book—it's a lifelong pursuit. **SUMIT** was designed to bring clarity to the vast worlds of business, psychology, philosophy, history, religion, and beyond. Each book distills the essence of profound ideas, influential figures, and transformative concepts, making them accessible and actionable for learners like you.

But why stop at one book? **Join the SUMIT Community** and become part of a vibrant network of curious minds dedicated to exploring and mastering the greatest ideas across disciplines.

Dive Deeper into your favorite subjects
Stay Inspired with insights from a growing library of expertly summarized knowledge
Connect with a community of learners who value growth and understanding as much as you do

Scan the QR Code Below to Join Us Today!
Together, we can continue to explore, learn, and create a legacy of knowledge that shapes our lives and the world around us. Don't just read about ideas—live them with the SUMIT Community.
(It's free, and you can unsubscribe anytime.)

Philosophy Summit Collection

Are you ready to explore the essence of wisdom and discover how great thinkers have shaped our world across centuries?

The Philosophy Summit Collection is your passport to a universe of philosophical ideas, bridging ancient and modern perspectives in a compelling, accessible way. Whether you're new to philosophy or seeking fresh insights, each volume in this groundbreaking series unpacks history's most influential schools of thought—revealing just how powerful these concepts can be for your everyday life.

Embark on your journey today, starting with our flagship title or any of the specialized volumes that catch your eye. It's time to climb the summit of thought and discover the heights of insight!

101 Philosophy Ideas - Timeless Wisdom to Empower Your Thinking and Your Life

Step into a fascinating introduction to philosophy that unites ancient wisdom with modern thought, giving you the ultimate roadmap to understand the history of philosophy and harness it for personal transformation. 101 Philosophy Ideas is your philosophy guide to the theories, thinkers, and debates that have shaped Western and Eastern philosophy alike—from Aristotle and Confucius to Nietzsche and beyond.

STOICISM Summarized
Ancient Wisdom for Modern Resilience: Mastering Mindset, Discipline, and Virtue for a Fulfilled Life

What if the secret to a powerful, unshakable mind was discovered over two thousand years ago? What if the path to true freedom, resilience, and success didn't lie in chasing wealth or external validation, but in mastering your own thoughts and actions? Are you ready to become Stoic?

EASTERN PHILOSOPHY Summarized
Timeless Wisdom from Hinduism, Buddhism, Daoism, and Confucianism for Mindfulness, Ethics, and Enlightenment

Transform Your Mind, Your Life, and Your Understanding of Reality! Are you ready to embark on a journey of transformation and insight? The path begins here.

EXISTENTIALISM Summarized
A Concise Guide to Freedom, Meaning, and the Absurd in Philosophy, Life, and Society

What does it mean to truly exist? Are we free, or are we trapped by forces beyond our control? If life has no inherent meaning, how do we create our own? This is more than philosophy—it's a call to action. Will you choose to live authentically? The abyss is staring back. Are you ready to stare back at it?

CRITICAL THINKING Summarized
The Ultimate Guide for Mastering Logic, Thinking Smarter, Spotting Lies and Making Better Decisions

We live in an era of misinformation, logical fallacies, and relentless persuasion—an age where half-truths spread faster than facts, and biased reasoning can lead entire societies astray. Critical Thinking Summarized is your weapon against deception, manipulation, and flawed reasoning.

ETHICS Summarized
Understanding Right and Wrong: A Complete Overview of Ethical Theories and Moral Reasoning

What is right? What is wrong? And why does it matter? From the dawn of civilization to the rise of artificial intelligence, humanity has wrestled with moral dilemmas that define our existence. Are you ready to think deeply, argue boldly, and challenge everything you thought you knew about morality?

PHILOSOPHY OF MIND Summarized
Exploring Consciousness, Free Will, AI, and the Nature of Thought

What is consciousness? Can we trust our perceptions? Do we have free will, or are we just complex machines running on neural code? If you've ever questioned reality, if you've ever wondered what makes you you—this is the book you've been waiting for.

POLITICAL PHILOSOPHY Summarized
Key Thinkers, Theories, and Debates on Power, Justice, and Freedom—From Plato to Postmodernism

What is justice? Who should rule? Can power ever be legitimate? This is no dry academic textbook. It's a bold, accessible, and razor-sharp and everything you need to master political philosophy—without the fluff, jargon, or confusion.. Understand the past. Decipher the present. Shape the future.

PHILOSOPHY OF RELIGION Summarized
A Concise Guide to Faith, Reason, God, and the Big Questions of Existence – Arguments, Critiques, and Key Debates in Religious Philosophy

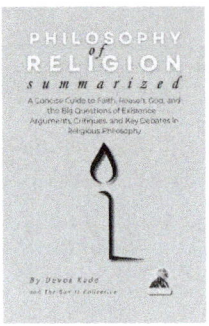

What is the nature of God? Can faith and reason truly coexist? Why do some find deep meaning in religion while others reject it outright? Is there a way to settle the debate once and for all?

ANCIENT GREEK PHILOSOPHY Summarized
A Complete Guide to the Thinkers, Ideas, and Legacy of Classical Philosophy—From Socrates to Aristotle and Beyond

What does it mean to live a good life? What is truth, and how do we find it? Can reason shape society, or is chaos inevitable? These are not just questions for scholars in ivory towers—they are the foundations of how we think, act, and live today. The wisdom of the ancients awaits.

NIETZSCHE Summarized
Understanding Nietzsche: A Clear Guide to His Most Powerful and Controversial Ideas

What if everything you believed about truth, morality, and human nature was an illusion? What if God were dead, and you were left to forge your own path in a world without absolute meaning? If you are ready to think dangerously, live courageously, and go beyond good and evil, then this book is for you.

Psychology Summit Collection

Unlock the secrets of the mind and drive your personal growth to new heights with the Psychology Summit Collection – a comprehensive library of psychology wisdom. This series brings together holistic analyses of psychology, cognitive science, and human behavior with concise reference guides, giving you the ultimate toolkit for understanding the mind and applying its lessons in everyday life. Whether you're a psychology enthusiast, a business professional, a student, or on a self-improvement journey, this collection will elevate your knowledge and empower you to influence behavior and achieve lasting change.

Start your ascent with the Psychology Summit Collection today – and become the master of your mind.

101 Psychology Ideas - Understand the Mind, Influence Behavior, and Achieve Lasting Change

What if you could crack the code of the human mind and use it to improve every aspect of your life? 101 Psychology Ideas is your ultimate field guide to understanding how minds work and applying psychology to influence behavior and spark positive change. Take the first step toward lasting change and empowerment.

FAMILY PSYCHOLOGY Summarized
The Ultimate Guide to Family Dynamics, Parenting, Relationships, and Mental Health—Insights for Stronger Bonds and Lasting Happiness

What makes a family thrive? Why do some relationships deepen over time while others fracture under pressure? How can you foster resilience, love, and emotional intelligence in your household?

MOTHER AND CHILD PSYCHOLOGY Summarized
The Science of Maternal Bonding, Child Development, and Parenting Strategies for Lifelong Emotional and Cognitive Growth

What makes a mother's love so powerful? How does early bonding influence a child's intelligence, resilience, and sense of self? Why do some children thrive while others struggle emotionally? Unlock the Science of Mother-Child Bonding

FATHER AND CHILD PSYCHOLOGY Summarized
The Essential Guide to Parenting, Attachment, and Child Development for Stronger Father-Child Bonds

What does it truly mean to be a father? How does a man shape the mind, heart, and future of his child? Drawing from the latest psychological research and timeless wisdom, this book delves into the essential role of fathers—from the earliest days of infancy to adulthood. Fatherhood is not just a role—it is a legacy. Start building yours today.

SOCIAL PSYCHOLOGY Summarized
The Ultimate Guide to Human Behavior, Influence, and Decision-Making – Master Social Dynamics, Persuasion, and Psychological Triggers

What if you could decode every social interaction with scientific precision? What if you could persuade, influence, and connect with people effortlessly—whether in business, relationships, or everyday life? Are you ready to unlock the psychology of influence, persuasion, and social dynamics?

COGNITION Summarized
The Ultimate Guide to Understanding the Mind: Theories, Processes, and Practical Applications of Cognitive Science

What if you could unlock the mysteries of your own mind? What if you could master the art of thinking, decision-making, learning, and creativity like never before? Unlock the secrets of cognition. Transform the way you think. Buy your copy today.

PERCEPTION Summarized
A Comprehensive Guide to Understanding Human Perception: How We See, Hear, Feel, and Interpret Reality Across Senses, Cultures, and Technologies

What if everything you see, hear, and feel isn't what it seems? Rich with insights into vision, hearing, taste, touch, memory, and more, this book doesn't just explain perception—it shows you why it matters. Uncover how perception defines your reality.

PERSONALITY Summarized
A Comprehensive Guide to Traits, Theories, and Self-Discovery for Personal Growth and Success

Unlock the Secrets of Who You Are and Who You Can Become. What truly defines you? Are you born with your personality, or does the world shape it? Can you change who you are—or are you destined to remain the same? Are you ready to take control of your personality—and your destiny? Start your journey today.

BEHAVIOURAL PSYCHOLOGY Summarized
The Ultimate Guide to Understanding Human Behavior, Conditioning, and Behavior Modification Techniques

Unlock the Secrets of Human Behavior and Take Control of Your Life! Why do people act the way they do? How can habits be broken, behaviors reshaped, and decisions influenced? Prepare to see the world differently. And more importantly—learn how to change it.

DEVELOPMENTAL PSYCHOLOGY Summarized
Essential Guide to Human Growth, Behavior, and Lifespan Development – Key Theories, Research, and Practical Insights

Unlock the Secrets of Human Development – From Birth to Beyond! Why do we think, feel, and grow the way we do? How do childhood experiences shape our future? What drives personality, intelligence, and emotions across the lifespan? Are you ready to decode the blueprint of human development? Start your journey today!

Religion Summit Collection

Embark on an enlightening journey across the beliefs that shape our world. The Religion Summit Collection is more than just a series of books – it's a personal voyage of discovery through the wisdom of ages. Each volume invites you to a "summit" of ideas where Eastern philosophies meet Western traditions, ancient teachings encounter modern questions, and curiosity sparks personal growth at every turn.

Join the countless readers who view the Religion Summit Collection as a must-have resource for expanding their horizons. If you long to connect the dots between faiths or seek wisdom to navigate your own life challenges, this series is your companion. Open your mind and heart to a summit of spiritual knowledge – and prepare to see the world's religions in a whole new light.

101 Religion Ideas - **Explore Diverse Traditions, Deepen Your Perspective, and Enrich Your Spiritual Life**

What if one book could open your mind to 101 profound insights from the world's great religions? 101 Religion Ideas is your gateway to understanding how centuries-old wisdom can empower and inspire your modern life. Unlock the wisdom of the world's religions – dive into 101 Religion Ideas today and embark on a transformative spiritual adventure.

CHRISTIANITY Summarized
A Complete Guide to the History, Beliefs, and Practices of the Christian Faith

For over two thousand years, Christianity has shaped civilizations, inspired revolutions, and transformed countless lives. But what is Christianity at its core? What do its followers truly believe? How did it evolve from a small group of disciples to the largest faith in the world?

ISLAM Summarized
A Concise Guide to Islamic Beliefs, History, Law, and Spirituality – Understanding Islam, the Qur'an, Shariah, Sufism, and Muslim Traditions

For over 1,400 years, Islam has shaped civilizations, inspired profound spiritual traditions, and influenced the course of world history. Yet, for many, it remains misunderstood—overshadowed by stereotypes and misconceptions.

BUDDHISM Summarized
A Complete Guide to Buddhist Philosophy, Teachings, and Meditation—From Theravāda to Zen and Tibetan Buddhism

For over 2,500 years, Buddhism has transformed the lives of millions, offering a path to inner peace, clarity, and awakening. But with its vast traditions, complex philosophies, and deep meditative practices, where does one begin? Are you ready to begin your journey?

HINDUISM Summarized
A Complete Guide to Hindu Philosophy, Scriptures, Gods, Rituals, and Spiritual Wisdom

Step into the vast, awe-inspiring world of Hinduism—a tradition that has shaped the spiritual consciousness of billions for over 5,000 years. This book is your gateway to understanding the profound wisdom, sacred rituals, divine deities, and timeless philosophies that define this extraordinary faith.

JUDAISM Summarized
Everything You Need to Know About Jewish Faith, Culture, and Tradition in One Essential Book

What does it truly mean to be Jewish? How has Judaism survived and thrived through centuries of exile, persecution, and renewal? Why do Jewish traditions, laws, and beliefs continue to shape the modern world? Understand Judaism. Appreciate its beauty. Engage with its future. Are you ready to discover the soul of a people?

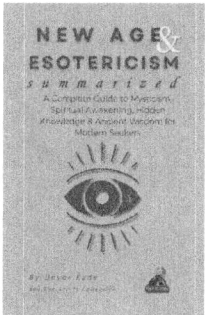

NEW AGE & ESOTERICISM Summarized
A Complete Guide to Mysticism, Spiritual Awakening, Hidden Knowledge & Ancient Wisdom for Modern Seekers

Are you ready to uncover the secrets of the cosmos, awaken your inner power, and transform your spiritual destiny? New Age & Esotericism Summarized is your ultimate guide to the mystical realms of hidden knowledge, ancient wisdom, and modern spiritual evolution.

TAOISM Summarized
Taoist Philosophy, Spirituality, and Practice for Inner Peace, Balance, and Enlightenment

For centuries, Taoism has remained an enigmatic and profound philosophy, whispering its wisdom through the Dao De Jing, the paradoxes of Zhuangzi, and the graceful movements of Tai Chi. But what if you could grasp its essence in one compelling, immersive volume? Walk the path. Embrace the flow. Live in harmony with the Tao.

COMPARATIVE RELIGION Summarized
World Religions, Beliefs, and Spiritual Traditions – Exploring Sacred Texts, Practices, and Theories Across Faiths

Religion shapes civilizations, ignites wars, heals wounds, and inspires revolutions. It weaves itself into the fabric of our existence, influencing how we love, how we fear, and how we understand the unknown. But what happens when we step back and examine it all—side by side? This is the book you've been waiting for.

MYTH & FOLK RELIGIONS Summarized
Exploring Legends, Myths, and Sacred Traditions Across Cultures – From Creation Myths to Shamanism, Folklore, and Urban Legends

Myths are more than ancient tales—they are the pulse of civilizations, the echoes of forgotten gods, and the whispers of ancestors shaping our world. From the trickster gods who defy order to the heroic figures who battle darkness, myths illuminate the human experience in ways both mystical and profound.

WICCA & PAGANISM Summarized
Exploring Witchcraft, Magic, Rituals, Spells, Wiccan Beliefs, and Ancient Pagan Traditions

Unlock the Mysteries of Wicca and Paganism—A Journey into Ancient Wisdom, Magic, and Spiritual Awakening! No fluff. No gimmicks. Just raw, essential knowledge—distilled into an engaging, accessible volume that will deepen your understanding of Wicca, Witchcraft, and Pagan traditions.

Business Summit Collection

A powerhouse series of business books delivering expert insights on entrepreneurship, business strategy, startups, and professional development. Designed for ambitious professionals, entrepreneurs, and aspiring business owners, this collection distills wisdom from top business minds and real-world success stories. Each volume in the series offers actionable guidance, proven strategies, and inspiring case studies – from launching innovative startups to mastering leadership and growth tactics. Whether you're looking to ignite a new venture or elevate your current business, the Business Summit Collection provides the knowledge and tools to thrive in the 21st-century business landscape. Join thousands of readers in discovering cutting-edge ideas and practical advice to drive your success.

101 Business Ideas – High Potential Businesses for the 21st Century

Looking to launch a successful business in today's world? 101 Business Ideas – High Potential Businesses for the 21st Century is your ultimate guide to turning inspiration into enterprise. This comprehensive book unveils 101 innovative business ventures across various industries.

MARKETING Summarized
Master the Art of Branding, Digital Strategies, and Customer Engagement in the Modern Era

Step into the dynamic world of marketing like never before! This isn't just another textbook—it's your ultimate guide to mastering the strategies, tools, and innovations that drive today's most successful brands. Unlock your potential.

ENTREPRENEURSHIP Summarized
The Complete Guide to Starting, Growing, and Scaling a Successful Business

This is not just another book about entrepreneurship—it's your blueprint for building something extraordinary, for breaking free from the ordinary, and for redefining what's possible. Are you ready to take the leap?

MANAGEMENT Summarized
A Comprehensive Guide to Mastering Leadership, Strategy, and Organizational Success

Unlock the Secrets to Mastering Leadership, Strategy, and Organizational Success. If you're ready to step into your full potential, lead with confidence, and create lasting impact, this is the book for you. Transform your career. Transform your world.

PROJECT MANAGEMENT Summarized
The Ultimate Guide to Mastering Agile, Risk, and Resource Strategies for Successful Projects

In the fast-paced world of business and innovation, project management is the superpower that transforms ideas into reality. Don't just manage projects—own them. Step into the driver's seat of your career, empowered with strategies that turn challenges into opportunities.

COMPETITION Summarized
Master the Fundamentals, Strategies, and Future Trends to Dominate Competitive Markets

In a world where every decision can mean the difference between triumph and failure, competition reigns supreme. From boardrooms to battlefields, from bustling markets to global megacorporations, competition drives progress, fuels innovation, and shapes the future of industries and societies.

HUMAN RESOURCES Summarized
A Comprehensive Guide to HR Strategies, Practices, and Trends for Success in the Modern Workplace

Unlock the secrets to mastering the art and science of managing people in today's dynamic business world. Perfect for professionals and newcomers alike, this is the one book your career — and your organization — cannot afford to miss. The future of HR is here. Are you ready to lead it?

PRODUCT DEVELOPMENT Summarized
A Comprehensive Guide to Creating, Launching, and Managing Market-Winning Products

Every groundbreaking product starts with a spark—but only those who master the journey from idea to market truly succeed. Are you ready to join their ranks? [...] This book will give you the edge you need to succeed in a fast-moving, competitive world. Don't just develop products—shape the future.

SUPPLY CHAIN Summarized
A Comprehensive Guide to Strategies, Analytics, and Innovations for Efficient, Resilient, and Sustainable Supply Chains

In a world where supply chains power every industry—from the gadgets in your hand to the food on your table—mastering the art and science behind them has never been more critical. Are you ready to transform challenges into opportunities and lead in the age of interconnected global commerce?

PRODUCTION Summarized
A Comprehensive Guide to Efficient Manufacturing, Lean Systems, and Sustainable Production for Business Success

A Comprehensive Guide to Efficient Manufacturing, Lean Systems, and Sustainable Production for Business Success [...] your blueprint for success. Your journey to production mastery begins here. Let's build something extraordinary.

OPERATION MANAGEMENT Summarized
Master the Fundamentals of Operations, Supply Chains, and Process Optimization for Business Success

Unlock the secrets to operational excellence and take your business to new heights! In today's fast-paced, hyper-competitive world, mastering Operation Management isn't just a skill—it's a necessity. Dive in today and lead your business to operational success!

Printed in Dunstable, United Kingdom

68817227R00107